Millstones &
Stumbling Blocks

Understanding Education in
Post-Christian America

Bradley Heath

FOREWORD BY
Thomas M. Askew

Fenestra Books
Tucson, Arizona

Millstones & Stumbling Blocks: Understanding Education in Post-Christian America

Copyright © 2006 by Bradley Heath
Published by Fenestra Books™
610 East Delano Street, Suite 104
Tucson, Arizona 85705 U.S.A.
www.fenestrabooks.com
Book design by Lori Sellstrom
Cover: Temple of Baalbec, Ruins of the Eastern Portico; by
Louis Haghe, after David Roberts; 1842.
Courtesy of V&A IMAGES / Victoria & Albert Museum,
London

Scripture taken from the NEW AMERICAN STANDARD
BIBLE ®, Copyright © 1960, 1962, 1968, 1971, 1972, 1973,
1975, 1977, 1995 by The Lockman Foundation. Used by per-
mission.

Cataloging-in-Publication Data

Heath, Bradley E, 1956-
Millstones and stumbling blocks – understanding education
in post-Christian America / Bradley E. Heath; foreword by
Thomas M. Askew
ISBN: 1-58736-556-1
LCCN: 2005936585
1. Public education–Evaluation and Criticism. 2.
Evangelicalism–United States. 3. History–Religious aspects–
Christianity. 4. Books and reading.

Advantage seems to favor
those from Gath,
For Christian education
is a path
Less traveled, due to rocks
along the way —
Stones slowly smoothed to
fit a sling someday.

For Adrielle, Audree, and Austin:
Arrows in our quiver,
Stones for His sling.

CONTENTS

FOREWORD

THIS BOOK IS addressed to the unconvinced, those who may have a problem referring to our nation's public schools as "millstones and stumbling blocks." It is also for those who may contend that the U.S. is not a "post-Christian" society. It is intrinsically a passionate book. Passion can be frightening, intimidating, exhilarating, or entertaining. I hope you will find that the passion which engendered this book is challenging, because it is passion tempered by wisdom and experience.

Brad Heath has earned the right to be heard on the subject of Christian education versus public school education. He rescued a failing Christian day school and administrated it for over four years, even though it was out of his comfort zone to do so. He recognized the poverty of his own educational background, and instead of cursing the darkness, he lit a candle. Twenty years later, his personal library has increased by 1,200 volumes. When a move to a new town provided inadequate educational options, he and his wife undertook the education of their own three children. His oldest daughter finished high school (at home) as a National Merit Finalist, and his second daughter was honored as a National Merit Commended Scholar. He incurred the wrath of the educational establishment in his small town by exposing the failure of the local public schools while opposing a tax levy for the local school system. He fiercely "cried in the wilderness" by writing letters to the editor of the local newspaper, and he signed

7

his own name. He got hate mail in return.

Mr. Heath was an able technical writer when I first met him twenty years ago. We often exchanged writing we had done as administrators of Christian schools in different cities. Over the years, a deeper and more thoughtful tone became detectable in his writing. Insightful quotations from a broad range of writers, skillful figures of speech, and an exquisite vocabulary began to mark his writing. My conclusion? "You've been reading the right books," I told him.

By his own admission, Brad Heath has not written an apologetic for the kind of Christian education he has devoted his life to providing for his children and others. Instead, he has climbed the wall to sound the watchman's warning for Christians who don't see the point in what he is devoted to, especially when there is a default alternative waiting at the nearest school bus stop. It would be easier (and more comfortable) to rest on his laurels, content in the personal accomplishments listed above. But on behalf of other Christians, he has read, researched, and spent laborious hours penning this warning about the failures of the American public school system.

If you are among the unconvinced, I entreat you to read this book with all critical faculties intact. If Mr. Heath has not built a clear and logical case for Christians withdrawing their support for government education, then feel free to sustain the status quo. But if he is speaking biblical wisdom, you must allow him to enflame your passions, just as his have become incensed by the realization that we Christians have been supporting an untenable situation.

And to the faithful "choir" who already "get it," you'll find lots of good quotables!

Thomas M. Askew, EdD
Headmaster, Cornerstone Christian Academy
Tucson, Arizona

PREFACE

Deliver those who are being taken to death,
  And those who are staggering to slaughter,
Oh hold them back.
  If you say, "See, we did not know this,"
Does he not consider it who weighs the hearts?
  And does he not know it who keeps your soul?
And will he not render to man according to his work?
                                    — Proverbs 24:11-12

THESE SOBERING WORDS are often applied to abortion, genocide, or famine — things we rarely, if ever, personally encounter. But, this troubling command, eerily foretelling our denial, also applies to the ordinary, common, and routine. Children on playgrounds and big yellow buses make me ponder this passage. These Scriptures can bring lip-trembling sighs to parents whose children have rejected their faith, and the feeble excuse — *See, we did not know this* — echoes from pulpits that neglect the biblical imperative for Christian education.

My criticisms of public education may seem unfair, unkind, or even un-American. How dare I criticize this enduring institution? Ironically, segregation and smoking once enjoyed the same social acceptance public schools now hold; the popular majority may favor foolish things. Although public schools are not completely bad, admiring them uncritically is like saying rattlesnakes have lovely

9

diamond-patterned skin. These schools are dangerous regardless of superficial attributes.

This is not a scholarly work, and I have intentionally highlighted only the most egregious public school defects. Legions of tenured education professors and other would-be reformers have filled many a book, journal, and PhD thesis with highbrow academic critiques. This book, however, is for moms and dads, regular folks who have a hunch that all is not well in the merry ol' land of education. Their parental instincts are correct; indeed, things are much worse than they imagine.

I am not criticizing specific people, but an inept bureaucratic system masquerading as the benevolent guardian of children. I contend that public schooling shamelessly betrays the children it claims to serve:

> And whoever receives one such child in My name receives Me; but whoever causes one of these little ones who believes in Me to stumble, it would be better for him to have a heavy millstone hung around his neck, and to be drowned in the depth of the sea. Woe to the world because of its stumbling blocks! (Matthew 18:5-7)

Thus, the premise of this book is simple: Public schools are stumbling blocks, not building blocks.

I am patient with those honestly ignorant of a Christian philosophy of education; heaven knows the church has not taught them one. I am growing admittedly impatient, however, with church leaders and maturing Christians who continue to suckle the lukewarm milk of compromise. British humorist Hector Hugh Munro captured my sentiment for such self-indulgent sensibilities: "I wouldn't mind writing a letter of angry recrimination or heartless satire to some suitable recipient; in fact, I should rather enjoy it, but I've come to the end of my capacity for expressing servile amiability."[1] Likewise, I am not writing to be amiable, nor am I writing to be contentious, combative, or controversial. I am writing so parents will realize the popular public school alibi—*See, we did not know this*—is sorely inadequate and dangerously negligent. Parental ignorance of public schooling definitely hurts children.

My thoughts and observations are not original, and I can think of no worse criticism for this book than these words: innovative, novel, revolutionary. I earnestly desire this book be imitative, so I may appear like a child on his father's shoulders—taller, stronger, and more capable than I really am. My contribution is like coffee whose most important ingredient is the additive, water. I have allowed the water of words to flow through me from a reservoir of books, conferences, and conversations. I have tried to brew a robust and refreshing cup, definitely not decaffeinated. I hope it wakes up some people.

Books about education fill entire libraries; it is not surprising this one is neither comprehensive nor complete. My writing reflects the brevity and focus with which I have necessarily addressed my topics. Robert Louis Stevenson once observed:

> The writers of short studies having to condense in a few pages the events of a whole lifetime, and the effects on his own mind of many various volumes, is bound, above all things, to make that condensation logical and striking. For the only justification of his writing at all is that he shall present a brief, reasoned, and memorable view."[2]

Thus, *logical, striking, brief, reasoned,* and *memorable* constitute my handful of adjectival ambitions for this book.

Finally, I offer a sincere warning: This is a hard book. The difficulties are not in its grammar, vocabulary, or concepts, but in its bold attack on the cherished cultural icon of public schooling. Consequently, my writing may seem intentionally confrontational to those who are intentionally complacent. This book presupposes blindness to the defects and dangers of public schooling. Removing scales from the eyes requires touching the eyeballs, always an uncomfortable proposition. Although the goal is better vision, the process may feel like a poke in the eye; the natural reaction is to close one's eyes and turn away.

I appeal to readers (whose children or sympathies now attend public schools) to give this book an honest hearing. My writing is aggressive based on the assumption that adults can confront vital issues without personalizing them. I write with intensity because I want people to think with intensity. Some Christians regard strongly-worded arguments as uncharitable, but good often comes from conflict. Disagreement plows the fallow ground of complacency and turns under the weeds of *status quo*. Disputes define. Conflicts clarify. While frustration, disagreement, or even anger, may be understandable reactions to this book, they do not justify quitting before finishing — hear me out before you throw me out.

CHAPTER 1

Fooled by the Familiar, Enamored by the New

All heaven and earth resound with that subtle and delicately balanced truth that the old paths are the best paths after all.
— J.C. Ryle

M Y EDUCATION WAS written with a public school pen, hardly qualifying me to critique the system. I am like a misspelled word complaining its author writes poorly. It is always awkward when the student criticizes the teacher or the ink rebuffs the pen. But, even spelling errors tell us something about their author. Although my educational deficiencies may impugn my credentials, they also implicate the public schools that inscribed them upon me. I am both a son and a cynic of public schooling.

I grew up in the Corn Belt where I now live an unusually ordinary and enjoyable life — wife, kids, job, small-town Americana. I was schooled as a technician for the information economy, and my illiberal education shaped my thinking a mile deep (technically) and an inch wide (philosophically). Since receiving this educational gash, I have endeavored to read as my sole—and perhaps soul—defense against the wounds inflicted by twelve years of public schooling.

Author and educator George Grant has aptly described the multitudes of poorly educated Americans: *They do not know that they do not know.* This was certainly my case as a freshly minted college graduate. Art, history, music, literature, theology, philosophy—all of these and more were missing from my education and my life. I knew science and mathematics, but even these had been taught as isolated "subjects" unrelated and detached from any universality. My schooling and my thinking lacked substance, integration, and context.

Initially from instinct and eventually from understanding, I sought different schooling options for my children. They attended a Christian school I helped administrate and were later home educated. The reigning public school professionals do not consider such educational dabbling to be book-writing credentials worthy of a merit badge. That is fine; I do not expect their approval, but an apology would be nice. As Dante pined, "Time that is lost displeases him the most that knows its worth!"[1] I am still piqued with them for leaving me deep in the woods without a compass.

The path out began with reading and led to an epiphany: I suddenly knew that I did not know... much of anything. Gradually, great books by great men began clearing debris from the trail of knowledge. I slowly came to recognize my chronological snobbery (as C.S. Lewis called it) and to resist the arrogance of modernity. I realized my generation was not the best and brightest to have walked the planet simply because we were the latest to have done so. I eventually discovered both the content and context of my public schooling were but shadows of the substantive education once normative for children in the West. I had been robbed of my educational heritage by the purveyors of a foolish, socially engineered, morally bankrupt, and politically correct public schooling system.

John Buchan, the great Scottish statesman, educator, and author, recounted our incredible educational legacy this way:

> Our greatest inheritance, the very foundation of our civilization, is a marvel to behold and consider. If I tried to describe its rich legacy with utmost brevity, I should take the Latin word *humanitas*. It represents in the widest sense, the accumulated harvest of the ages, the fine flower of a long discipline of Christian thought. It is the Western mind of which we ought to turn our attentions to careful study.
>
> The now frivolously disregarded *Trivium*—emphasizing the basic classical scholastic categories of grammar, logic, and rhetoric—once equipped untold generations of young pupils with the essential tack and apparatus for a lifetime of learning. These are the very notions that once set acourse the great cultural flowering of Christendom over the past thousand years.[2]

Modern public schooling is the wall-mounted trophy head of a formerly lionhearted education. Its truncated and life-less hulk provides a tamed likeness of the once vibrant and powerful creature whose pursuit exhilarated the hearts and minds of countless students. To be the prey of such learning was to be mauled by beauty, truth, and good-ness; to stalk it to its lair was an expedition fraught with danger and delight. Sadly, the taxidermists of modernity have done their work well. Public schooling is a hollow shell, a stuffed charade, a glass-eyed cadaver of the once substantive education preceding it. Public schooling is a poor imitation of true education—an inert imposture that is rigid, posed, and dead.

While public schools boast of using the latest technolo-gies to teach an abundance of scientific facts, multicultural

15

trivia, and basic life-skills, the culmination of their effort is knowledge without wisdom and facts without truth. In contrast, Buchan believed true education steadfastly affirms: "Every student, every family, every community, and every nation needs to be grounded in the good things, the great things, the true things in order to do the right things."[3] Beauty, truth, and goodness are the heart and soul of genuine education and their absence has shriveled public schools into educational wraiths.

Historically, western education thrived in the consensus of Christian thought and practice permeating cultural, commercial, and political institutions. The absence of public schooling during the unprecedented millennial rise of Christendom is evidence of a broader and more effective context for education. Tutors, private academies, church schools, home education, vocational associations, and professional apprenticeships now seem anachronistic in the face of a monolithic public schooling system. Yet, education has been neither improved nor empowered by homogenizing it through a system of universal public schools. Public education has mass-produced schooling as a commodity, but it has essentially destroyed education as a community.

Education is both taught and caught; it is both content and context. Hence, education is most fruitful when its *content* is imparted in the *context* of a sympathetic and symbiotic community. In her insightful book, *Heirs of the Covenant*, educator Susan Hunt makes this point well:

> The content and the context of the covenant are woven together in Scripture, and they must be delicately woven together in the education of God's people. So this education is both cognitive and experiential. It is formal and informal. It is head and heart. It must get into the mind and the muscles.[4]

In other words, the content of education must be validated

by the context in which it is presented. Context confirms content. Therefore, a child's educational community — parents, teachers, friends, church, school, and family — should be living confirmation of the content being imparted.

The irrelevance of God is a fundamental doctrine taught by all public schools. What I was taught and what I caught from public schooling were overwhelmingly in conflict with my faith community. Is the Bible true? My science, health, and literature teachers said no. Is God providential in the affairs of men and nations? My history, social studies, and economics teachers said no. Is there design and purpose evident in creation? My biology, chemistry, and math teachers said no. Are there absolutes? My sex-education teacher said no and my friends said "cool." Is God relevant to any subject taught in public school? All of my teachers and all of my books said no. Consequently, every day for twelve years the *content* and *context* of my public schooling said there is no God, and even if there is, He does not matter.

Granted, some of my public school teachers privately professed to be Christians, creating a dichotomy between what they taught and what they really believed. Eventually, I realized they were paid to follow the public school script (whether they believed it or not) and what was taught in class was often half-truth. Other teachers were true believers in the public school content; one would think they were eyewitnesses to a Darwinian fish crawling out of the primordial ooze. They delighted in tearing down what they considered the antiquated mores of my pastors, parents, and Sunday School teachers. They were at least consistent with the curriculum. Ultimately, I learned these lessons from my public school teachers: Faith is private, subjective, and compartmentalized. Truth is relative, situational, and individualized. The greatest virtues are openness, tolerance, and diversity, and the worst wrong is to think you are ever right.

Perhaps the last sentence should read, "The worst

wrong is to *think.*" Why? Thinking is the least taught discipline in public schooling. The stifling conformity of their educational methodology stamps out one cookie-cutter student after another. Public schools are structured like factories — mass-producing a one-size-fits-all educational commodity — and operated like prisons, complete with medical sedation, metal detectors, video surveillance, and SWAT team hostage drills.

By emphasizing mental mass-production and social standardization, the public schooling factories have nearly achieved the efficiency of a high-speed Coca-Cola bottling plant. Legions of children are conveyed rank and file through a serpentine course of closely prescribed processes. They are socially aligned, washed of cultural contaminants, sanitized of spiritual sensibilities, and filled with a carefully prescribed formula (purportedly a secret recipe known only to the social engineers in teacher colleges and text book publishing, but rumored to contain large doses of openness, tolerance, and diversity). Finally, they are capped at a graduation, labeled with a diploma, and sent out to teach the world to sing in perfect harmony.

Public schools are so busy indoctrinating children with *what to think* they fail to teach them *how to think*. With characteristic prescience, G.K. Chesterton described the advent of our muddled modern thinking of which public schooling is a great engine:

> The great intellectual tradition that comes down to us from the past was never interrupted or lost through such trifles as the sack of Rome, the triumph of Attila, or all the barbarian invasions of the Dark Ages. It was lost after the introduction of printing, the discovery of America, the coming of the marvels of technology, the establishment of universal [public] education, and all the enlightenment of the modern world. It was there, if anywhere, that there was lost or impa-

18

tiently snapped the long thin delicate thread that had
descended from distant antiquity; the thread of that
unusual human hobby: the habit of thinking.[5]

Why do we tolerate and even embrace public schooling? Being a public school product makes *thinking* critically
about them very difficult. It is hard to criticize the familiar,
friendly, and fraternal. John Taylor Gatto, New York State
Teacher of the Year, acknowledged this mental paraly-
sis in his provocative book, *Dumbing Us Down*: "It is the
great triumph of compulsory government monopoly mass
schooling that among even the best of my fellow teachers,
and among even the best of my students' parents, only a
small number can imagine a different way to do things."[6]
Doing things differently requires thinking things
through for ourselves. We must carefully consider the
educational philosophies and methodologies shaping our
children. What content? What context? Imparted when,
where, how, and by whom? Regrettably, many Christian
parents allow public school "professionals" to think for
them. We inadequately consider the issues and surrender
our thinking and children to the experts—a poor choice in
light of Wilfred McClay's humorous observation: "Thinking, like lovemaking, changes its character dramatically
when it's turned over to the professionals."[7]
Public schooling *is* seductively alluring: facilities,
sports, technology, academics, entertainment, enrichment, and socialization, all conveniently packaged and
readily available on a nearby street corner. Yet, we must
resist the seduction of these polished professionals. Do
the public educationists really know what is best for my
child? Do career bureaucrats, curriculum boards, and the
textbook industry really have my child's best interest at
heart? Should the state dictate the content and context of
my child's education? Is education primarily a parental or
governmental responsibility?
In his influential book, *Standing on the Promises*,[8] Doug

Wilson summarizes the case for not sending children to public schools. He reasons that Christian parents are morally obligated to keep their children out of public schools because:

- The Scriptures expressly require a non-agnostic form of education (Deuteronomy 6:4-9).

- Keeping the greatest commandment requires that we love God with all our minds (Matthew 22:37).

- God expects parents to provide for and support their children.

- Sending children into an intellectual, ethical, and religious war zone without adequate training and preparation is a violation of charity.

- The declared intellectual goal assigned to the church in Scripture is to pull down strongholds, arguments, and every high thing exalting itself against the knowledge of God (2 Corinthians 10:4-5).

- The continued presence of Christians in public schools subsidizes a lie and keeps an institution dedicated to false teaching in existence.

Unlike Wilson, I am not writing an apologetic for Christian education. I am alerting Christian parents to the seductive charms and fraudulent claims of public schools. Many parents make poor educational choices because, as Professor Allen Bloom observed, "They lack what is most necessary, a real basis for discontent with the present and awareness that there are alternatives to it."[9] I am also confirming parental intuition (that gut-level feeling something is wrong) and encouraging informed educational choices.

Understanding the public schooling paradigm also requires the examination of our culture, our churches, and ourselves. We are not the autonomous, self-made individuals we imagine. Family heritage, faith communities, and popular culture inevitably shape us, as do historical movements, social philosophies, and emerging technologies (e.g., The Enlightenment, evangelicalism, post-modernism, automobiles, computers, and television to name a few). Why we do what we do resides in these micro- and macro-influences. Consequently, our beliefs and lifestyles are often inherited, inhaled, and ingested. Unfortunately, they are also often unexamined.

This book challenges the seldom-questioned ideology of public schooling and attempts to dismantle its popular persona. It also questions the cultural assumptions and dubious practices of many evangelicals who enthusiastically support these schools. Some Christians will find this offensive because it challenges their unexamined beliefs and casually accepted notions. Nevertheless, I am yelling *fire!* because so many families are succumbing to educational smoke inhalation, beginning as a sweet-smelling savor but ending with third-degree burns.

I may offend readers who think sounding the alarm is worse than the fire itself. If so, I apologize, for I have no intention of condemning parents for their educational choices and I realize some parents have few options. I am, however, also unwilling to falsely reassure them. Public schooling will burn your kids! It is out of concern, not condemnation, that I sound the alarm and strike the smoldering schoolhouse door with a verbal fire-axe. The point is rescue, not recrimination.

If you are sympathetic to public schooling, please keep reading. If you are also sympathetic to Christian families, realize this book is meant to help them. All schooling choices are not equal, and some are more biblical than others. How we educate our children is a very serious matter, and our choices should stand the scrutiny of careful examination, whether or not the light hurts our eyes.

The apostle Paul gave Christians a strong warning:

"See to it that no one takes you captive through philosophy and empty deception, according to the tradition of men, according to the elementary principles of the world, rather than according to Christ" (Colossians 2:8). Tragically, this is exactly what public schools are doing to children and parents alike. I cannot remain silent while such educational neglect and abuse continues. The squandering of our spiritual, cultural, and intellectual legacy must stop. We must not sentence another generation of children to the dreary twilight of the post-Christian mind.

There is one sense in which my writing is meant to inflame; I am trying to light a signal fire—a lantern, a beacon, a lighthouse. Although this book is only a matchstick in the raging blizzard of educational confusion, I hope its igniting flash and sulfur smell will kindle a blaze bright enough to signal those lost in the storm. Perhaps striking this match will startle some drowsy soul to ask: "What was that?"

CHAPTER 2

Things We Would Rather Not Know

In order to discover the line of our duty rightly, we should take our children in our hand and fix our station a few years further into life; that eminence will present a prospect, which a few present fears and prejudices conceal from our sight.

— Thomas Paine

THIS BOOK IS for Christians, and as a sign of the times I must define the term. I do not restrict it to the narrow definition of American evangelicalism — those who pray a particular prayer. I do not expand it to include all who are baptized into the church; the sheep and the goats both get wet. Repentance and baptism may initiate the Christian life, but I describe "Christians" as those who acknowledge their obligation to the truth-claims of the Bible. These Christians not only profess saving faith, they demonstrate it through obedience to God's Word. They are doers and not merely hearers (James 1:22).

Although I write to Christians, I do not assume a sympathetic audience. Many evangelicals will find this book an uphill climb because it challenges their commonly held beliefs and practices. I know this because I have spent decades living and learning this book in the context of the evangelical community. I realize many dedicated Christians do not "get it" when it comes to education. Yet, their educational wounds cannot be healed lightly. This book is not meant to tickle their ears, but to passionately convey the biblical imperatives and cultural implications inherent in how they educate their children. It may cause discomfort, strong words, like strong medicine, often do.

When considering criticism, watching for inconsistent logic and false arguments is wise; we should always think and question when reading. I am admittedly critical of public schooling, and some may think my points are exaggerated or invalidated by their own experience. Although I readily admit the public school plague has various symptoms (not every school has a shooting), I am resolute that their pervasive malady is an unwavering commitment to secularism—universally held, religiously practiced, and judicially enforced. This malignancy has metastasized into a variety of New Age and humanistic pathogens. Indeed, public schools are fertile ground for nearly every ideology and philosophy except biblical Christianity. The disease manifests differently from school to school, but all are infected, contagious, and frequently fatal to Christian faith.

Many Christians do not consider public schooling a battleground for their children. The warfare is deceptively waged by the familiar and comfortable. We are disarmed by homey Norman Rockwell images of book-laden boys shuffling down the lane to school and freckle-faced girls in calico reciting spelling lessons. Many parents irrationally cling to a sentimental visage of public schooling (a sort of Anne of Green Gables, one-room schoolhouse), while the reality is closer to images invoked by Columbine, Paducah, and Leavenworth.

Some parents worry about the public school environment, but concern over the unlikely chance of our children being physically assaulted should pale in comparison to the certainty of assault on their Christian faith and beliefs. It is not the improbable violence to their body but the assured violence to their mind and spirit that constitutes the clear and present danger of public schooling. Few Christian parents have lost their children to public school violence, but multitudes have lost their kids spiritually, intellectually, and philosophically by ignoring the real threats these schools pose.

Christian parents are reticent about discussing public schooling. The problems are complex and seem an unnecessary distraction from the monumental task of rearing a family. Many of our family, friends, and fellow Christians are public school teachers or students, and most of us are products of this ailing system. There is a perceived reality of public schooling as an American institution in which failure to participate is deemed almost unpatriotic. It seems risky to draw the ire of education bureaucrats by pointing out their failures. Others have pleasant school memories: favorite teachers, sports, cheerleading, prom, clubs, activities, and just hanging out with friends. Some are convinced their kids should be "salt and light" in the public school wasteland. Our church leaders offer little or no objection to public schools, so why should we?

These factors make criticizing public schools an uncomfortable endeavor. It is much easier to surrender to the relative safety of silence. Why rock the boat? Why be an alarmist? After all, as a pastor once told me, God is everywhere so He cannot be kicked out of public schools. God is, of course, present in public schools in the same sense that He is present in crack houses and brothels. But His Word is neither present nor presented in public schools. His truth is not taught in these schools. Christianity is not welcome in these schools. God is not honored, obeyed, or even acknowledged in these schools. Yes, God is in public schools, like the night shift janitor — out of sight and out of mind.

Make no mistake; the much-touted neutrality of public schooling is a myth. Public schools cannot and do not teach math, science, history, literature, or anything else with a neutral unbiased objectivity. Every fact is an interpreted fact. Every fact has an underlying frame of reference and an accompanying set of presuppositions. For example, if you believe there is no God, will you reach the same conclusions when teaching biology or history as someone who acknowledges the existence of a providential Creator? What if, in the name of neutrality, you do not deny God, but instead never mention Him as relevant to anything studied during twelve years of public schooling? Does that silence matter? Does it send a message? Is reducing God to irrelevance acceptable and without consequence? Can you lock God in a Sunday-only box of personal choice and expect this educational schizophrenia to have no ill effect?

Those who believe the myth of neutrality tell Christian parents to handle religious issues at home. Such spiritual segregation is unbiblical because, as Susan Hunt observes, Christians are called to live unified and integrated lives:

> Our covenant relationship with God is to be the unifying principle of life. Our faith is to be integrated into all of life. No thing and no time is outside the scope of this all-encompassing reality. Life is not to be compartmentalized.[1]

State and federal laws countermand this unity by requiring public schools to practice institutionalized agnosticism. God must be shut out. By silence they declare God irrelevant and unimportant in every area of life and study. Public schools illegitimately operate as God-free zones claiming exemption from the lordship of Christ. This is not neutrality. This is bias, contempt, and rebellion against God's Word; this is twelve years of atheism.

Public schooling is non-Christian by design. Its frame

26

of reference, its interpretation of facts, and its educational philosophy are intentionally non-Christian. Again, this does not make public schools neutral. They are no more neutral than a Buddhist school, an Islamic school, or a Communist school. They simply offer a different non-Christian education; they do not offer neutrality.

Even so, many evangelicals mistakenly ascribe neutrality to public schools because we live compartmentalized lives ourselves. By defining religious activity as what happens on Sunday mornings between 10:00 A.M. and noon, it never occurs to us that what happens Monday through Friday between 8:00 A.M. and 4:00 P.M. is also inherently religious. All schools are religious schools. All schools teach worldview. All schools have a philosophy of education. All schools have creeds, liturgy, and dogma. All schools have orthodoxy and doctrine. In short, all schools — public, private, parochial, and home — are enculturation centers, and none are neutral.

The religious nature of public schooling helps explain our reluctance to criticize it. It seems mean-spirited to critique the beliefs and actions of others. We are understandably uncomfortable criticizing someone else's religion, but the inherently religious nature of public schools should also help Christians understand the urgency to leave them. Would we disapprove of Islamic schools if Christians were taxed to support them and compelled to attend them? Would we remove our children from such schools? I hope so. All education is inescapably religious. The existence of non-Christian schools is not the problem; Christians using them to train their children is the issue. Christian children need Christian education.

Ideas have consequences. What we believe determines how we live. Or if you prefer, "For as he thinketh in his heart, so is he" (Proverbs 23:7). The harsh truth is that public schooling is anti-Christ, literally against Christ. Public schools substitute man for God in their explanations of all things. The creator God is swept away in the spiral of evolutionary progress; His providential acts are explained as random chance and "survival of the fittest." The secularism taught in public schools is diametrically opposed to Christianity. They are as different as night and day, and inflicting these lies on Christian children is a foolish thing.

Education is not a pragmatic question of what works. Even if pigs could fly and all public schools had excellent academics, they would still be no place for training Christian children. The issue is one of obedience to the educational principles clearly set forth in Scripture. Public schooling derails the biblically-mandated training of children, and leads them to reject the virtues, faith, and praxis of their then-astonished parents.

The Southern Baptist Convention (SBC) has 16 million members and constitutes the largest evangelical denomination in America. Retired USAF Brigadier General, T.C. Pinckney, serving as the SBC Second Vice President, recently addressed their executive committee with these sobering words:

> We are losing our children. Research indicates that 70 percent of teens who are involved in a church youth group will stop attending church within two years of their high school graduation. Think about that statement. It addresses only teenagers who attend church and participate in the youth group. What does that suggest about those teens who may attend church but do not take part in the youth group, or who do not go to church at all? In a talk at Southwestern Seminary Josh McDowell noted that less than one-third of today's youth attend church. If he is right and 67 percent do not go to church and then we lose 70 percent of those who do, that means that within two years of finishing high school only 10 percent of young Americans will attend church. We are losing our youth.[2]

To be fair, these devastating statistics cannot be blamed solely on the unbiblical educational model practiced in public schools. Christian parents and evangelical churches share the greatest culpability for their incredible naivete in expecting good fruit from bad trees. "You will know them by their fruits. Grapes are not gathered from thorn bushes nor figs from thistles, are they? So every good tree bears good fruit, but the bad tree bears bad fruit" (Matthew 7:16-17). Not surprisingly, the rocky, barren, nutrient-deficient soil of public schooling yields tares and thistles; Christians should know better than to try growing wheat there.

Many concerned parents are now trying Christian education with the caveat that they can always return to public schools if it gets too hard or costly. This is similar to entering Christian marriage with the conscious thought that one will get a divorce if things do not work out. Christian parents should see choosing public schooling as analogous to choosing divorce: a grievous, heart-breaking decision made only as a last resort. Public schooling is simply the wrong choice for Christian families. We should not line up at the public school trough just because the swill is familiar, convenient, and free.

Despite overwhelming evidence, many people deny public schooling is a threat to children. Amazingly, public schools remain a cultural icon and are nearly as hard to criticize as a New York City firefighter after 9/11. Nonetheless, we must abandon our raw allegiance and sentimentality if we are to rescue survivors from the smoldering rubble public schooling has made of American education.

Of course, public schools see themselves as messiah, not pariah. These self-appointed nannies of cultural well-being *know* what is best for American children; just ask them. Although public schools miserably fail teaching reading, they have limited success with brushing, flossing, and washing behind the ears. This approach — education as life-skills — gets more interesting than swish-and-spit when schools begin teaching children how to avoid the germs found in the back seat of a car instead of those lurking on the drinking fountain.

Germs may be bad, but the arch nemesis of the health-and-welfare curriculum is the evil demon of smoking. Therein a fragrant irony rises from their burning indignation against tobacco, for smoking is perhaps the best metaphor for public schooling.

Smoking was once widely accepted (before its dangers were known), and cigarettes were the embodiment of sophistication in movies, television, and advertising. To previous generations, smoking might besmirch your teeth but not your character; alot of folks lit up without worrying about cancer, emphysema, or nicotine addiction. Smoking was a cultural norm, just as public schools are now. Indeed, these schools are as popular and unquestioned as smoking once was. Unfortunately, they are also as hazardous and habit forming.

Addicted smokers like to justify their habit with exceptions, pointing out a geriatric chain-smoker still going strong at ninety. Public schools do the same by heralding the relatively few students who succeed in spite of widespread failures. Such self-satisfied boasting mimics an infamous cigarette advertisement that once cooed, "You've come a long way, Baby."[3] Public schooling has certainly come a long way, down a path of foolishness and failure.

Those who monitor our educational health repeatedly warn us of the adverse side effects and harmful risks these schools pose. Student achievement and well-being continue to decline as the government schools inhale deeply from the fag of scholastic experimentation, social engineering, and moral relativism. It is no wonder this secondhand smoke sickens so many children.

Public school proponents argue like big-tobacco lawyers that they are not responsible for the academic and social maladies suffered by children using their product. Like cigarettes, public schools should have a warning label:

> *SURGEON GENERAL'S WARNING: Public school-ing may be hazardous to your mental, spiritual, and physical health. Use of this product has been shown to promote ignorance, indifference, and immorality in school age children.*

Even so, I am not criticizing smoking or education in general. The abuse of a thing is no argument against its right use; tobacco and education are not exceptions to this rule. Let me clarify, however, that I am NOT pro-moting smoking, lest the anti-smoking zealots take my comments as a burly endorsement and target me in their prohibitionist purge.

Many parents who would be aghast over tobacco smoke in their children's lungs think nothing of educa-tional smoke in their brains and hearts. Someone who well understood this foolishness said it this way: "Not what enters into the mouth defiles the man... But the things that proceed out of the mouth come from the heart, and these defile the man" (Matthew 15:11, 18). In other words, children face a far greater danger from how public schools shape their hearts and minds than they do from "Smokin' in the Boys' Room."

Tobacco's risks may outweigh its benefits; yet, respon-sible and infrequent consumption could be defined as proper use. Likewise, proper use of education requires a content of beauty, truth, and goodness conveyed in a con-text of knowledge, understanding, and wisdom—about as likely to be dispensed in a public school classroom as unfiltered Camels and a Zippo.

The comparison of public schooling and smoking shows broad social acceptance is no measure of the ben-efits or risks of either. Being a cultural norm is not the same as being good for you. Excessive smoking is abuse of tobacco; public schooling is abuse of education. When it comes to education, attending public schools is like smoking a pack a day.

CHAPTER 3

Teaching Is Evitable, Learning Inevitable

A pupil is not above his teacher; but everyone, after he has been fully trained, will be like his teacher.

— Luke 6:40

C.S. LEWIS (WHOSE pencil I am unworthy to sharpen) clarified the public school conundrum in his essay, "On the Transmission of Christianity."[1] To paraphrase him, the problem is not that public schools do not work, but that they work all too well. They masterfully reproduce their beliefs, doctrines, and philosophies in the minds and hearts of impressionable children who inevitably learn these lessons. This really should not surprise us, for it is a law as universal as gravity: "Then God said, 'Let the earth sprout vegetation: plants yielding seed, and fruit trees on the earth *bearing fruit after their kind* with seed in them;' and it was so" (Genesis 1:11, emphasis added). The principle is as old as Eden. Students become like their teachers, and fruit does not fall far from the tree.

Children are teachable by design. Many first graders passionately exclaim, "My teacher says . . . " followed by something for which they have no objective data or life experience except that whatever "Ms. Smith" says must be right. Kids are wired to think this way. Nevertheless, public educationists would have us believe that teaching children is incredibly complex and difficult—certainly not to be tried at home by parental amateurs!

The rise of the expert and demise of the parent have dramatically affected education. Unlike tutors and private schools hired directly by parents, public schools have less connection and little accountability to the family. Public schools do not function as an extension of the Christian home or serve *in loco parentis*. Public schools are first and foremost agents of the state, which considers children its property to be instructed *in loco rei publicae*—in the place of the state. The voice of the customer (parents) is unintelligible to a learning industry that arrogantly believes it knows best, regardless of what parents actually want.

Public educators no longer see themselves as journeymen passing on established knowledge through proven methods. They now fancy themselves "professionals" who experiment on children using the ever-evolving science of education, while abandoning the tried-and-true methodologies of the past. In short, public schooling is an experiment and children are the guinea pigs.

Despite these modern pretensions, the honorable and respectable occupation of teaching is most accurately classified as a highly-skilled craft. Children are neither machines nor computers, and the mere transfer of data and skills is not education. Good teachers master the tools of learning and use them to shape minds and *hearts*. They train their students to wield these tools for themselves as apprentices in the pursuit of knowledge, understanding, and wisdom. Regrettably, the arrogant professionalism of many public educators further alienates parents from the education of their children, which they are now deemed unqualified to direct. Such didactic professionalism does, however, help explain the epidemic of inflated self-esteem among public school students: They learn it from their teachers.

Although public schools feign anxiety over student achievement, they actually benefit from the criticism that children are not learning. The continuing "crisis" in American education is a windfall. Poor academic achievement is fueling incredible funding for salaries, staffing, facilities, curricula, and technology. It is commonly held — in the mythology of public schooling — that children are not learning what they are being taught. In reality, they *are* learning what they *are* being taught. They are taught not to read, so they learn not to read. They are taught not to write, so they learn not to write. They are taught to think like the world, so they are learn not to think like Christians. As C. S. Lewis observed, the problem is with the teaching, not the learning:

> If we had noticed that the young men of the present day found it harder and harder to get the right answers to sums, we should consider that this had been adequately explained the moment we discovered that schools had for some years ceased to teach arithmetic. . . . If the younger generation have never been told what the Christians say and never heard any arguments in defense of it, then their agnosticism or indifference is fully explained. . . . There is nothing in the nature of the younger generation which incapacitates them from receiving Christianity. If any one is prepared to tell them, they are apparently ready to hear. . . . The young people today are un-Christian because their teachers have been either unwilling or unable to transmit Christianity to them.[2]

The childlike faith of young students appears to become more discriminating over time, but not because children become less teachable. They simply learn different lessons from their teachers. They learn skepticism because they are taught to doubt. They learn openness because they are taught relativism. They learn unbelief because they are taught unbelief. And so it continues, while their own fallen natures add fuel to the tempting lessons offered by their teachers. This shaping process is inescapable. The consistent correlation between what kids are taught and what they learn means public schools are best judged not by what they claim to teach, but by what students actually learn. Output reveals input.

Although genius and dunce may not fit this pattern, vast numbers of students are eminently teachable and learn their lessons very well. This begs the question of the often-dismal academic performance found in public schools. The answer is children cannot learn what they are not taught; likewise, they have indeed learned what they were taught. They are taught not to read. They are taught not to spell. They are taught not to write. They are taught not to know history, English, and geography. Ultimately, they are taught not to love learning, and they learn that lesson all too well. Whether children are learning is never in question; it is always what are they learning — what are they being taught?

Many Christians wrongly assume public schools are about the business of transferring neutral information from the teacher's brain to the child's. Naive parents think education deals only with objective, measurable, indisputable facts. Nothing could be further from the truth. Learning does not take place in a sterile environment free of contamination or catalyst. Education is not unbiased; every fact is an interpreted fact. Every idea is spun upon a web of presuppositions and related assumptions. Teachers, curricula, and school ethos all contribute to a process of education that is nothing less than the imparting — no, imparting is not a strong enough word — nothing less than the *enculturation* of a worldview. G.K. Chesterton said, "Education is not a subject and does not deal in subjects. It is instead a transfer of a way of life."[3] But if so, what are some of the presuppositions of modern public schooling? What kind of life do public schools transfer to children? Russell Kirk described it well:

> The popular notion that the revelations of natural science, over the past century, somehow have proved that men and women are naked apes merely; that the ends of existence are production and consumption merely; that happiness is the gratification of sensual impulses; and that concepts of the resurrection of the flesh and the life everlasting are mere exploded superstitions. Upon these scientistic assumptions, public schooling in America is founded nowadays, implicitly.[4]

Given these presuppositions as their pedagogical framework, public educators will never lead children to Christian virtues, though they will lead legions of little ones away from the faith. Amazingly, many pastors and parents believe Sunday School is an effective antidote to the godless indoctrination received in Monday-through-Friday school. A daily drenching in public school will not evaporate in an hour of Sabbath sunshine.

American Christians place far too much confidence in their children's baptism or recitation of a sinner's prayer; not nearly enough emphasis is placed on biblical parenting and discipleship. Christians who would never send their children to a Jehovah's Witness VBS or enroll them in an Islamic day school have few qualms about the heresies dished up daily in public schools. Yet, these schools intentionally teach their children doctrines antithetical to Christianity.

All schools are in the disciple-making business; it is what they do. Public schools do not teach children to think like Christians, but they certainly teach them to think like the world. University of Chicago professor Allen Bloom described the cause and effect of public schooling in his provocative book, *The Closing of the American Mind:*

> Every educational system has a moral goal that it tries
> to attain and that informs its curriculum. It wants to
> produce a certain kind of human being. This inten-
> tion is more or less explicit, more or less a result of
> reflection; but even the neutral subjects, like reading
> and writing and arithmetic, take their place in a [pre-
> meditated] vision of the educated person. . . . There
> is one thing a professor can be absolutely certain of:
> almost every student entering the university believes,
> or says he believes, that truth is relative. The danger
> they have been taught to fear from absolutism is not
> error but intolerance. Relativism is necessary to open-
> ness; and this is the virtue, the only virtue, which all
> primary education for more than fifty years has dedi-
> cated itself to inculcating.[5]

In other words, the cumulative effect of twelve years of
public schooling is that many children reject the faith of
their fathers and embrace openness, diversity, and tolerance in the most pejorative use of those terms. Such
consequences do not stem from inevitable adolescent
rebellion, but are the cultivated fruit of children who have
learned the lessons taught in public school.

Evangelicals often accept or reject behavior using a
simple litmus test: Is it a sin? There are, however, many
permissible things that should be moderated. The Amish
provide an interesting example. They will ride in cars but
not own or drive them. They will use telephones and watch
television but allow neither in their homes. They will light
their rooms with oil lamps but not electric lights. To modern evangelicals, the Amish appear either hypocrites or
fools, but the Amish do not restrict cars, telephones, and
electricity because they believe these things are sinful.
They restrict them because they correctly perceive them as
threats to their lifestyle and culture. They have thought-

fully considered the impact technology has on their lives and the on the *way of life* they are transferring to their children.

I am not promoting a neo-Amish or Luddite philosophy. Technology is a God-given tool for dominion we must learn to handle wisely; sin resides in the human heart and not in objects and technologies around us. From the Amish, however, we can learn to be intentional and thoughtful about our Christian lifestyle. We need not throw out the TV, but we must recognize the harm in too much television—a problem not solved by substituting Veggie-Tales for R-rated movies. If our children are more enamored with visual entertainment (television, computers, and video games) than with the printed word, we have not understood the power and influence of visual media or moderated them appropriately. If our teenagers are withdrawn from family life and captivated by their multi-media players and cell phones, we have not used those technologies wisely.

Similarly, we must carefully consider the powerful and permanent effects education has on our children. We are starting with the wrong question when we ask: Is it a sin to attend public school? Better questions are: How will public schools disciple my children? How will public schools influence the lifestyle and worldview I am transferring to my kids? How will the *content* and *context* of public schooling mold my son or daughter? How will public schools honor the lordship of Christ in the education of my children? When we have contemplated the answers to those questions in light of the biblical mandate to provide our children a thoroughly Christian education, the first question about "missing the mark" has an obvious answer.

Because the anti-Christian bias in public schooling is often subtle and implicit, many parents think it is also harmless. These moms and dads may get concerned when teachers start handing out condoms, but they do not bat an eye when secularism saturates every book and class.

Yet, C. S. Lewis warned it is the subtle, not the obvious, which is most dangerous:

> Our faith is not very likely to be shaken by any book on Hinduism. But if whenever we read an elementary book on Geology, Botany, Politics, or Astronomy, we found that its implications were Hindu, that would shake us. It is not the books written in direct defense of Materialism that makes the modern man a materialist; it is the materialist assumptions in all the other books.[6]

Likewise, it is the secularist assumptions in all expressions of public schooling that stunt the souls of Christian children, shriveling them with unbelief. Few teachers, particularly in elementary school, directly denounce Christianity. They do not have to; the content and context do the work for them. By the time many kids graduate high school, they are well down the road of disregarding and discarding their Christian faith. Some will still call themselves Christians, but their definition is based on a subjective spiritual experience — they threw a pinecone in the fire at youth camp — and not on the objective tenets of the Christian faith, an integrated affirmation of a biblical worldview, or the evidence of spiritual disciplines. In short, public schools have trained them to be Christian secularists — unbelieving believers.

Ken Myers has suggested an important corollary to C. S. Lewis's warning about subtle non-Christian assumptions: Students will find Christianity most plausible and compelling when their education is infused with latent Christian assumptions. In other words, if all subjects are implicitly based on Christian presuppositions, students will learn to think biblically. Regrettably, public schools forbid this integration.

It is difficult to recognize the bad when it is cloaked in the seemingly good. It requires that we look beyond immediately apparent conditions to cumulative effects and long-term consequences. If we focus on a given public school in a given year, we may correctly conclude the fourth grade teacher is a fine Christian woman who works hard and loves her students. Or, perhaps, we will conclude the superintendent of schools, the school board president, and the elementary principal are all well-respected leaders, active in their churches, and prominent in the community. We may also find the school district does well on state proficiency tests. But, if we enroll our children for these reasons we have reached a wrong conclusion and made a bad decision.

This paradox — the apparent goodness of public schooling — is precisely why so many Christians do not "get it." After all, they reason, Christian virtues are also manifest in the common grace and civility found in the larger culture, including public schools. Christians are called to disciple the nations through loving, serving, and teaching others, so public schools seem like a good fit. Some really wonderful Christians work in public schools, so why criticize them? This is a fair question, which this entire book addresses.

The short answer is that my criticisms are not aimed at individuals, but at the unbiblical educational system they serve. Nevertheless, real people run these institutions. One would not have to look far to find flesh and blood examples who intentionally labor in public schooling to advance their personal vision of the world. Yes, Virginia, there are true believers (in secularism, feminism, relativism, socialism, "gayism," scientism, environmentalism, etc.) and many of them write textbooks, serve on school boards, teach in classrooms, or administer public schools.

Most evangelicals do not understand that neutrality is a myth and all education is inherently religious. We barely see these principles when considering overtly religious schools; so we are all but blinded by the fraudulent claim of impartiality in public schools. Worse yet, public schools borrow lumber from the Christian worldview to veneer their godless ethos. They like the smooth, rich finish of Christian character—love, joy, peace, patience, kindness, goodness, faithfulness, gentleness, and self-control—but detest the necessary blueprint, framework, and crafts-manship. Consequently, they produce some students who outwardly resemble the handiwork of genuine Christian education, but inwardly have the moral fiber and world-view consistency of particleboard—a hodge-podge slurry of relative values held together by the glue of openness.

Public schools pry slats from the Christian fence because the finished product of their own subjective secu-larism is untenable. They have clear-cut the timber and burned the hardwood—beauty, truth, and goodness—from the educational landscape leaving little behind except a wasteland of relativism and despair. They still encour-age a nondescript, generic moralism (tolerance, openness, and diversity are popular themes), but any thinking stu-dent should immediately ask: Why? By whose standards? By what authority? Says who? When students reject the arbitrary answers given to these questions, public schools must hide their shoddy workmanship behind a facade of respectability stolen from Christianity. As more Christians withdraw their kids from public schooling, the barrenness of its godless secularism will be increasingly apparent.

A few Christian teachers sprinkled among twelve years of agnosticism may give students fond memories, but they will not give them a biblical worldview. Educa-tion has content. They teach children "truth" and by state law truth is overtly secular and explicitly non-Christian. They also implicitly teach philosophies and *isms*, burning aromatic, ideological incense children innocently inhale as secondhand smoke. It is amazing how many public school children worry about global warming, rain forests, and saving the whales. It is little wonder they grow up to wor-ship the creation rather than the Creator.

The boards of education and school administrations

are also culpable. They goad taxpayers into building ineffective educational bureaucracies and shamelessly exploit children to perpetuate their funding—it's for the kids. The worst of them are modern-day Pharisees who covet community prominence and pontificate on the messianic nature of their schools. These blind guides, spawned from the public schools they champion, lead others into pits that neither sees (Matthew 15:14).

Granted, most public school employees are not true believers on a crusade to change society. They are nice people, trying to make a living, who do not understand the machine they operate or the agenda it advances. Such happy ignorance allows them, with disarming sincerity, to appear as social servants. Yet, they are unwittingly the functionaries of secular ideologues who control the sociological and philosophical content of public schooling. Many teachers and staff are just running the railroad. The final destination and condition of the cargo is not their primary concern; they are just earning a living.

Parents who find comfort in ever-elusive school district proficiency scores should be realistic. After all, the fox is guarding the hen house, and it is hard to hit a moving target. In every state, the department of education grades local public schools with a biased and vested interest in the outcome. The bar is set low, and the proficiency criteria are changed regularly lest concerned parents and taxpayers catch on. Parents who are impressed because a public school satisfies all the state requirements have no idea how diluted the standards are. They are called *minimum* standards for a reason.

What if public schools had wonderful academics? Is there consolation in knowing some schools occasionally produce secular scholars and erudite unbelievers? Is it comforting that some students can become both mental giants and moral midgets? What will these graduates bring us . . . human cloning, genetically-enhanced designer children, or pharmaceutically-altered personalities? Will they become the politicians who restructure our social order by redefining marriage, family, and sexuality? Will they expand the abortion cultural to the open acceptance of infanticide and euthanasia? Will they wantonly exploit our human and environmental resources pursuing economic gains?

The future promises unprecedented technological progress — science as savior. Who will govern its application? What will guide the ethical and moral judgment of men and women steeped in the agnosticism and relativism of public schooling? Will they be a law unto themselves or, perhaps worse, instruments of an imperial state? Can the intellectual, financial, and scientific elite be kept in check by a less gifted and poorly educated populace? Will the typical public school graduate have the wisdom to understand the issues, protect his liberties, and fulfill his responsibilities? Can the poorly educated remain free? History suggests not. The twentieth century — the first with universal public education, the fastest in scientific advancement, and the bloodiest in human history — is a frightening harbinger.

Enculturation is central to education. Our children are shaped — heart, soul, and mind — by their schooling experience. As Ken Myers wisely observes, "Schools and the structure of schooling orient the affections of our children."[7] Christian parents are morally obligated to orient the affections of their children toward the true, the beautiful, and the good, which requires biblically consistent *content* embodied in the *context* of an affirming faith community. This godly orientation is what Christian schools and home education provide — enculturation via Christian content and context. Public schools provide enculturation via secular content and worldly context, and the resulting orientation and affections are completely different. The schools we choose will inevitably shape our children and ultimately shape our world.

CHAPTER 4

Rise Up, O Men of God

Knowing is not enough; we must apply. Understanding is not enough; we must do. Knowing and understanding in action make for honor. And honor is the heart of wisdom.

— Johann von Goethe

CHRISTIANS OFTEN HAVE a foxhole mentality: Keep your head down and mind your own business. This may be a successful defensive strategy in the short term, but it is wholly inadequate in the long-term mission of proclaiming the gospel and extending Christ's kingdom. In a secular society, biblical Christianity will always appear countercultural. Although we merely want to be left alone (to worship our God, raise our families, and educate our kids), rejecting prevailing cultural norms is often perceived as confrontational and controversial. Our quiet obedience can be a thundering witness.

On the other hand, imitating unbelievers by enrolling our children in the same public schools accomplishes little. When Christians educate their children in the same manner as non-Christians, they send an undeniable message of agreement with non-Christian values, beliefs, and practices taught in public schools. Conformity does not witness to the lost, but falsely reinforces their unbelief. Instead, Christians should reflect God's grace and truth by demonstrating biblical alternatives to the bankrupt philosophies around us. We cannot throw a lifeline to those drowning in godless secularism if we are treading water in the same swamp. We must be different.

It is not easy to say the Emperor's new clothes are missing when our whole culture seems convinced his invisible finery is . . . Oh, so beautiful! But, it is vital that Christians expose the nakedness of secular thinking, especially when it masquerades in the respectable name of educating children. The biblical injunction to be "salt and light" in a dark and unsavory world is not fulfilled by embracing the public school but by engaging the public square. We are responsible to give an account for the hope within us, and this includes being able to explain and demonstrate our principled rejection of public schooling. Presenting a gracious antithesis to the secular confusion around us is a bold and necessary witness.

Christian education is not a matter of individual opinion or personal preference; it is an obedient response to the clear and unambiguous instruction of Scripture. Parents who substitute a godless public education for a thoroughly Christian one are ignoring the explicit counsel of God's Word. There is no educational neutrality. Again, choosing a public school is no different than choosing an Islamic school, except the Islamic school is not agnostic.

The Bible does not give a chapter-and-verse prohibition, "Thou shall not send your kids to public school." It even tells us that certain men of God survived similar experiences; Joseph and Daniel come to mind. But, we should never willingly sell our children into Egyptian slavery or purposefully exile them into Babylonian captivity. It is one thing to be *forced* into a pagan culture and atheistic education; it is quite another to embrace it through convenience, apathy, or neglect.

Some may wonder why more Christian leaders have

not openly called for an exodus from public schools. Regrettably, many pastors are clueless about the dangers of public schooling, while those who do understand are often afraid of the conflict and alienation that comes from taking a stand. Thus, sermons on Christian education are few and far between, and the risk of offending church members whose families attend or work in public schools is deemed greater than giving tacit approval to their unbiblical worldviews. To be fair, some pastors diligently treat the infectious heresies and spiritual maladies contracted through public schooling. It would be far better, however, if Christian children were not immersed in this virulence in the first place.

The "technicality" of having no eleventh commandment explicitly prohibiting the use of public schooling is a sad defense for poor biblical exegesis. Notable passages, such as Deuteronomy 6 and Ephesians 6, clearly make Christian education a biblical imperative and parental responsibility. Yet, many evangelicals ignore such Scriptures or make private interpretations: *The Bible does not tell me how to school my kids.* Superficial dismissals are all too common among those who prefer an autonomous, unexamined life instead of biblical obedience. The Bible *does* tell us how to educate our children, and we ignore it to their peril. There is more to child rearing than making schooling choices, but if those are made poorly the rest is in jeopardy.

Historically, strong church and family leadership produced distinctively Christian culture. Papas and pulpits were the cultural and educational prow prior to ubiquitous public schools. Unfortunately, many churches now emulate secular culture, and many fathers surrender their leadership to experts and interlopers. As a result, irony abounds. For example, many churches create stunning youth ministries hoping to strengthen kids, while simultaneously endorsing the morally-corrupting public schooling system—the ultimate youth ministry. This is like opening windows to let smoke out of the kitchen, yet leaving the frying pan smoldering on the fire. Public schools and youth ministries are often two branches of the same pop-cultural tree, and hapless parents who trust them to disciple their children are left wondering why the fruit smells funny.

Admittedly, this type of educational demarcation begs tough questions: What about single moms who cannot home educate or afford Christian school? What about Christian kids who do not want to leave public school friends? What about Christian parents who are public school teachers and administrators? What about Christian parents who want their kids in public school sports or fine arts? What about pastors who do not understand, encourage, or support Christian education? What about families who can afford Christian education for some, but not all, of their kids? What about Christian parents who think *their* public school is an exception? What about . . . ?

These rhetorical questions acknowledge real world issues. Who says obedience is easy? There are, however, biblical answers to these situations, though too few seek them. The questions we should be asking are: What about the Word of God? What are the consequences of disobedience? What are the benefits of obedience? What blessing or cursing am I bringing upon my family through my response to the biblical mandate for Christian education?

Unfortunately, some Christians inadvertently contribute to the befuddlement surrounding this issue. Their attitudes and actions are too schismatic toward fellow Christians who still support public schooling. Instead of providing a loving, patient, and understanding explanation of their principled decision for Christian education, they rudely and callously condemn their brothers for failing to see the light. Abrasive, judgmental parents make many pastors protective of public schooling. There is no place for arrogant self-righteousness concerning a decision for Christian education. Except for the grace of God and the revelation of His Word (neither of which result from human merit), our own children likewise would be perishing in public schools. It is not because we are meritorious; it is completely because God has graciously allowed us to glimpse His truth and mercifully blessed our awkward efforts to walk it out.

Nevertheless, our spiritual warfare against the public schooling system is something quite different, and we do not owe public schools the same deference we owe our Christian brothers. We are to cast down every high thing exalting itself against the knowledge of God (2 Corinthians 10:4-5). Therefore, we must recognize and treat public schooling for what it is—a modern-day Tower of Babel. We should take every opportunity to expose its failures, ridicule its follies, and discredit its image. Of course, this should be done by speaking the truth in love as Jesus did when addressing the Pharisees. We should follow His example when speaking truth to error. The one thing we must not do, however, is simply remain silent while yet another generation of American children is robbed of its cultural, intellectual, and spiritual inheritance. As Abraham Kuyper warned:

> When principles that run against your deepest convictions begin to win the day, then battle is your calling and peace has become sin; you must, at the price of dearest peace, lay your convictions bare before friend and enemy, with all the fire of your faith.[1]

War metaphors make many Christians nervous because we think if we are nice enough everyone will like us, or at least leave us alone. Many peace-mongering Christians espouse this sorry strategy, and legions of evangelicals have joined their group hug and deserted the cultural battlefield. Of course we can have peace, if we assimilate into the culture and become indistinguishable from it, keeping our faith silent, secret, and submerged. Sure we can avoid the cultural storm, if we scuttle the ship and sink quietly to the bottom.

Evangelicals are poor cultural strategists because our only battle plan is evangelism. We reject cultural engagement unless it coincides with witnessing. The dominion mandate (Genesis 1:28) is largely ignored due to a steroidal emphasis on soul-winning and an anemic understanding of eschatology. We find the notion of developing distinctively Christian culture unimportant and unnecessary as an end in itself, and we surrender cultural expressions to unbelievers as ground not worthy of the fight. Evangelicals worry far too much about being *left behind* and not nearly enough about what they are *leaving behind* as a cultural and spiritual legacy for future generations.

Ken Myers has made salient observations on this point. First, he says the challenge before evangelicals is not just unbelief, but how to believe — what does a faithful Christian lifestyle and culture look like? Secondly, Christianity involves the redemption *of* our humanity and not redemption *from* our humanity. Thus, cultural alertness, deliberateness, and engagement are important for culture's sake, not just for evangelism. As Myers comments:

> If Christian faithfulness were only a call to evangelism by whatever means possible, then capitulation to the spirit of the age (whatever it might be) might not be that serious. But since we are called to make evident the consequences of our redemption in every sphere of life, the Church cannot afford to be culturally complacent or careless. If the culture around us is committed to abandoning or thwarting the true, the good, and the beautiful, we are not obliged (out of some sense of evangelical winsomeness) to join the party.[2]

The road to a distinctively Christian culture has ditches on both sides. Many Christians veer into cultural apathy —

simply not caring; they retreat into an evangelical enclave safely cloistered from cultural interaction. Others drop onto the soft shoulder of hoping to win the lost by embracing non-Christian cultural expressions. Regrettably, the pursuit of cultural relevance has brought many questionable practices into the church; it is easy to lose control of these influential non-Christian cultural forms.

Christians are rightly concerned about culture, but they must learn to wisely engage it. Ken Myers again hits the mark:

> Precisely because we value politics, education, the arts, science, and all aspects of human life, we must not allow them to be held captive to dubious assumptions or agendas. When we adopt the disordered ways of the world we are not really loving our neighbors. Jesus enjoined his disciples to be wise as serpents and harmless as doves; he never suggested that they go out as sheep in wolves' clothing in order to increase market share.[3]

Christian cultural engagement is encumbered by the diversity of cultural expressions. The word *culture* now appends itself like a computer virus to almost every philosophy, institution, and entitlement group. We have corporate culture, academic culture, youth culture, gay culture, military culture, drug culture, popular culture (and its many Hollywood subcultures: television, music, literature, movies), feminist culture, welfare culture, environmentalist culture, Internet culture, liberal culture, conservative culture, sports culture, Christian culture, Islamic culture, Jewish culture, Hispanic culture, Black culture, Euro-centric culture, and on and on *ad nauseam*. The list does not end; America, like yogurt, is full of active cultures.

The length of the list is not the problem, but rather that evangelicals have failed to discern the incompatibility of various cultural expressions with those of biblical

Christianity. Our casual acceptance of many unbiblical philosophies and lifestyles is often due to ignorance of biblical worldview. Because we do not know what the Bible teaches, we fail to structure our lives in a distinctively Christian manner. This ignorance, however, is not a lack of theological understanding or doctrinal definition. Rather, it is the failure to embody our doctrines in an intentional community of shared stories, shared symbols, shared practices, and shared answers. Evangelicals need to be more intentional about the content and context of their faith—we need to be more Amish.

Many competing cultural claims are incompatible with biblical faith and practice, and Christians should not waste time cultivating these weeds. Instead, we need to strategically supplant non-Christian cultural claims with distinctively Christian alternatives. Some cultural expressions are compatible with Christian thought and practice, and we should infuse them as "salt and light." Public schooling, however, is emphatically not one of these, and attempts to reform it are ignorantly misguided.

CHAPTER 5

School Reform:
Dress Codes for Strip Clubs

*Christian education is not simply a matter of starting class with
Bible reading and prayer, then teaching subjects out of secular
textbooks. It consists of teaching everything, from science and
mathematics to literature and the arts, within the framework of an
integrated biblical worldview. It means teaching students to relate
every academic discipline to God's truth and his self-revelation in
Scripture, while detecting and critiquing nonbiblical worldview
assumptions.*

—Charles Colson

I OFTEN HEAR it argued Christian children should stay in
public schools and influence them for Christ. After all,
how can they be "salt and light" if we cloister them in
a distinctively Christian education? This reasoning is so
twisted it loops back to almost sounding right. Ironically,
the sorry state of public schooling has been achieved with
a majority of Christian families still enrolled. We are living with the daily result of Christian children being "salt
and light" in public schools; they are merely whitewash
on these educational sepulchers.

Only the desperate or delusional would send children

to fight a war—including the culture war in which public schools are secularist training camps. Christian kids are largely clueless about what is being done to them daily and yearly in the public school trenches. Their naivete and conformity are understandable because they have been rightly taught from kindergarten to trust and obey their teachers. Most students are helplessly unaware their Christian beliefs are being slowly and systematically deconstructed. This atmosphere of engrained trust and familiarity is fertile soil for supplanting biblical truth with secular ideology.

Evangelicals are notorious for fighting symptoms while perpetuating root causes. We have an uncanny knack for boldly attacking the wrong things in the wrong ways. It is amazing to watch Christian parents lead the PTA, champion school tax levies, and volunteer in classrooms; all of which inadvertently help public schools kidnap their children. "What! An educational crisis?" You can count on Christian parents to jump into the fray and grab the snake by the tail.

Ken Myers has wisely observed that not all social structures and institutions can be redeemed. It is impossible, for example, to be a Christian communist or a Christian hooker. The presuppositions of communism and prostitution cannot be reconciled with those of Christianity; one must yield to the other. Likewise, training Christian kids in public schools is simply laboring to produce "Christian" secularists; the predictable results are often three letters short of an oxymoron.

Public schools cannot be leavened by Christian involvement. As Doug Wilson correctly states, the government has designed the public school to be "an officially agnostic, tax-supported institution of education for dependent children."[1] This does not make schools neutral; it makes them non-Christian—a structural reality not overcome by Christian children infiltrating public school classrooms.

This has not stopped misguided evangelicals from

trying to manipulate public schooling. For instance, the growing debate over theories of origin—evolution versus intelligent design—gives evangelicals a lever to pull. In an odd role reversal, proponents of intelligent design are met with the same vitriolic jeers Galileo once received for saying the planets rotate around the sun. The scientific data is irrelevant to modern "flat-earth" evolutionists who shout down venerable colleagues, demanding they recant or face excommunication. The reigning scientific papacy wants no part of this emerging Copernican revolution, and being in power allows them to thwart unwelcome Christian encroachment. Thus, state courts and school boards are busy defending public schools from the dangerous heresy that life is not an accident.

Yet, they face a stubborn question: How did we get here? Some scientists attribute life to chance, that is, to random primordial events implying no transcendent purpose or meaning. They cannot *prove* how we got here, but they think it was an accident. Other scientists theorize that the complexities of life show evidence of purposeful and intelligent design. They cannot *prove* how we got here either, but they think it was no accident. Thus, some scientists speculate evolution is the only objective theory, while others consider intelligent design legitimate.

Arguably, both *theories* have scientific merit, but they are philosophically irreconcilable. Therefore, many courts and school boards see evolution as the only politically correct position because the notion of a cosmic "designer" is incompatible with legally agnostic public schools. Although evolution theory lacks scientific *proof*, it is philosophically compatible with public school dogma.

This raises the ire of many Christians who are now trying to force intelligent design into science standards. Unfortunately, these well-meaning reformers are also ignoring the nonsectarian nature of government schools and missing the main point—*public education is not Christian*. Once again, Christians are showing their incredible ignorance of first principles and their amazing ability to not get it. They are mobilizing grass-roots campaigns that, if successful, will be akin to establishing dress codes for strip clubs.

Predictably, strident evolutionists have attacked intelligent design as a thinly veiled attempt to impose religious faith on public schooling. Christians, however, are not alone in bringing religiously held beliefs to the debate. This is inevitably a faith issue for both sides: Evolution and intelligent design both require faith.

Public schools do not teach science from a biblical perspective, but this is merely the tip of the agnostic iceberg. They also do not teach math, music, history, literature, economics, art, or anything else from a Christian worldview. The slow sanitizing of Christian concepts from all subjects has not made public schools faith-free zones. Rather, explanations about the origin, purpose, and destiny of man are inherently philosophical, and the answers always require faith. The question is not whether we will have faith. It is always what we will have faith in.

All schools *religiously* teach worldviews of who we are, how we got here, and how we should live. Some schools derive these doctrines from holy men and holy books; others get them from sociologists, psychologists, and politicians. Christian schools seek to infuse education with transcendent truth, biblical absolutes, and moral virtues. In contrast, public schools emphasize relative values and social doctrines of diversity, openness, and tolerance. In either case, the education offered has a philosophical bias — the content is never neutral.

Public schooling is nonsectarian by law, that is, non-Christian, non-Muslim, non-Jewish, and so on. Complaining that public schools are not Christian is like saying that Christian schools are not Muslim. Of course public schools are not Christian; they are not intended to be. Christians are wasting their time, money, and children trying to reform public schools. Instead of imposing modesty on the public school dancers, Christians should quit going to these strip joints. Parents who want a Christian philosophy of education should never send their children to public schools. The evidence of intelligent design may exist, but sending your children to schools that teach the antithesis of your faith is not it.

Many Christians wrongly believe public schools were once intrinsically Christian and want to restore them by imposing Bibles and prayer on the classroom. Though it is true public schooling once gave lip service to Christian catechism, Scripture, and prayer, it is not true these schools were ever intentionally or explicitly Christ centered. The early religious expressions in American public schooling were often a nondescript Unitarianism, offering a highly-diluted faith of the least common denominator in service of a generic god. There is ample evidence public schooling was originally designed to free children from the shackles of religious superstition and antiquated Christian morality. Horace Mann, Stanley Hall, and John Dewey were not Boy Scouts or choirboys; public schooling once appeared to be Christian only because the prevailing culture actually was.

David Hegeman describes culture as, "the concrete expression of a society's religious and philosophical commitments."[2] His definition is an elaboration of Henry Van Til's aphorism, "culture is religion externalized."[3] The systemic secularism now externalized in public schooling is a reflection of the religious agnosticism endemic in the broader culture. Consequently, forcing Bibles, prayers, and creation science on public schooling is like baptizing the Mafia — evangelicals might feel better, but the crime wave continues unabated. A pervasive secularism has become the externalized religion of post-Christian America, and it cannot be changed by legislation.

Christians should not waste their time or talents trying to reform public schooling. The sooner this secular educational experiment collapses the better. We should remember compulsory government schooling is a relatively new invention and work to see it pass quickly into history as yet another failed utopianism. Christians cannot reform public schools, but we can fulfill our responsibilities as citizens and taxpayers to hold government agencies accountable.

Public schools are government schools. They are prone to fraud, waste, and abuse common in large, centralized bureaucracies. Christian citizens should demand financial accountability and oppose tax levies because the schools they fund conflict with their beliefs. Evangelicals protest loudly when their tax dollars fund abortion, but are strangely silent when their taxes abort godly education. Frankly, the perennial yard sign plea — It's for the kids — is a shameless political manipulation; the corresponding ballot should be routinely and decisively marked *no*.

Some Christians may even run for the school board. This should only be done in obligation to taxpayers and never because your children are actually in the system. The primary role of such board members should be whistle-blower and antagonist, not a task for the faint-hearted. Christians who harbor false hopes public schooling can be reformed need not waste their time on school boards. Schools have always been run by that mentality; there is no shortage of board members willing to spend someone else's money to perpetuate the problems.

In communities all across America, the best and brightest have presided over decades of uninterrupted, educational decline. School boards are no match for professional educationists and their entrenched bureaucracy. These boards provide "a facade of respectability and familiar faces to the clumsy apparatus of public instruction," but do nothing to correct the educational deficiencies stunting the minds and souls of American children.

The most effective educational reform is never to enroll your children in public schools. Beyond that, parents have the right as citizens and taxpayers to work for the diminution and eventual elimination of government schooling. It has taken nearly 150 years to build the public schooling empire, and it may take as long to dismantle it. The best long-range strategy is to render public schools unnecessary by developing Christian alternatives. We should start and support various forms of Christian education and encourage families to use them or home educate.

All societies legislate morality; every law represents a moral standard and definition of right and wrong. Legislating biblical standards works well in an overtly Christian culture; indeed, it was normative for centuries in America. Legislating Christian morality, however, would be incongruent in predominantly Muslim countries like Saudi Arabia, Yemen, or Iraq. As previously noted, culture is religion externalized. Christian prayers, Bible reading, and the Ten Commandments cannot be legislatively imposed when the broader culture (the externalized religion) and its institutions are thoroughly non-Christian. You cannot Christianize a Muslim country — or a secular one — by legislative mandate. Thus, the misguided evangelical hope of retaining a Christian America through legislation is woefully inadequate and destined to defeat. Hard work must actually be done to build a distinctively Christian culture in hearts and minds. This cannot be imposed by legislative fiat against the will of a rapidly growing, non-Christian population.

Many evangelicals believe America is a Christian nation, but indisputable evidence indicates America has entered a post-Christian period. A broad Christian consensus no longer informs or transforms our culture, our institutions, or our lives. Christianity has been privatized and marginalized into a wispy-thin vapor of individual spiritual experience. American churches — their shallow sectarian streams trampled by modernity and post-modernity — have become disembodied, effeminate therapy-centers for the pursuit of personal pietism, felt-needs, and self-realization. In short, American Christianity lacks verve, vigor, and vitality.

Evangelicals have always believed these criticisms about their uptown brethren in mainline denominations. We easily dismiss the historical church as mired in an orthodoxy of liturgy, liberalism, and lifelessness. But, it is evangelicals who are largely responsible for our current cultural impoverishment. Although they often admit they are adrift, evangelicals seem unconcerned about finding their position on the cultural seas. They do not know where they came from, where they are, or where they are going. Never have the saved been so lost.

Evangelicalism's cultural confusion is demonstrated by its inordinate affection for public schooling. Evangelicals do not understand what is wrong with public schools because they do not understand what is wrong with the church. Ironically, many churches are introspective and willing to change, but their market-driven innovations exacerbate the problems instead of solving them. Like the public school, the evangelical church frequently reinvents itself, and usually with disregard for precedents or predecessors.

Christians face a much bigger job than the red herring of public school reform. We face the incredibly difficult task of cultural reform, a job that begins with the church itself. Public schooling is an easy scapegoat because it accelerates our cultural decay. Nonetheless, public schooling is not the primary cause of post-Christian America; this fault lies squarely with the church. We must look to the church if we hope to diagnosis the disease and effect a cure.

CHAPTER 6

Christian-Lite:
Tastes Great, Less Fulfilling

Whenever we have an experience of direct, personal access to God, we are tempted to think and act as if we can dispense with doctrine, sacraments, history and all other superfluous paraphernalia of the church — and make our experience the sum and soul of our faith.

—Os Guinness

WHEN PASTORS START talking about issues hitting close to home, evangelicals are fond of saying they have gone from preaching to meddling. We like to hear strong, powerful sermons . . . when they are aimed at other people. Likewise, when an evangelical author critiques the church we are naturally cautious, if not skeptical. Constructive criticism is, however, exactly what I am offering. Why? Because evangelicalism and public schooling are genetically linked; indeed, they are distance cousins not fully understood apart from their familial ties. Take this assertion at face value for now, but I hope to prove it over the next few chapters.

The connection between public schooling and evangelicalism requires a deeper explanation of why the *state of the church* is directly related to the *church of the state*. Although the latter is clandestinely the public school, it is important to first understand the state of the church before assessing its civil counterpart. Despite the cultural misperception of the church as insignificant and irrelevant, it is (by God's design) the epicenter of human life. Consequently, examining evangelicalism is an elaboration on the theme of this book.

One of the great responsibilities of the church is educating and equipping God's people, including the covenant nurture of Christian children. Christ specifically sanctioned this by taking them into His arms and declaring the kingdom of God to belong to such as these (Matthew 19:14). Unfortunately, evangelicals have largely surrendered this responsibility to public schooling. Children spend more time as disciples of public schooling than in the active nurture of church and family combined. Their prolonged sentence is served under the tutelage of paid professionals whose concerted efforts and intentional agenda orient their young hearts, minds, and souls. Public schooling is often the strongest shaping influence in a child's life.

It is one thing if the responsibility for providing our children a thoroughly Christian education is usurped from church and home by, say, a communist state. It is quite another if this responsibility is voluntarily surrendered by church and home in the United States. Although classroom subjects might vary (Communism 101 vs. Capitalism 101), the premise of godless secularism underlying a North Korean public school is the same as its counterpart in North America. There is something dreadfully wrong when the church, without compulsion, pushes its children into the arms of a secular state to be nurtured, discipled, and trained. We know why this happens in China, but why is this practice common among American evangelicals?

To be sure, many churches employ full-time children's pastors and invest heavily in Sunday School programs and youth groups, usually resulting in a compartmentalized education that reduces the church's role to Bible stories and devotional ditties. Meanwhile, "real" education encompassing everything else is served up at the public school down the street. But, you will not find biblical truth on their menu. They do not serve Christians, and force those seeking a biblical worldview to the back of the big yellow bus. Religious discrimination is alive and well in public schooling.

Barring duress or dysfunction, it is simply unnatural for Christian parents to give their children up for educational adoption to the state. This is common practice among evangelicals, however, who apparently believe government schools are the best option for bringing their children up, "in the nurture and education *(paideia)* of the Lord" (Ephesians 6:4). Why else would one do this? Regardless of the reason, it is a weak church that subrogates the state to fulfill the obligations God requires of His people.

Yet, I am not telling you what to think about evangelicalism, its particular denominations, or your local congregation. Instead, I am focusing on why evangelicals think the way they do, and exploring how evangelicals have been shaped intellectually, spiritually, and culturally. These are important issues because they influence our thoughts and actions regarding public schooling. Put succinctly, I do not want to argue about the decision to paint the church chartreuse. I want to talk about why it is our favorite color.

To cover this ground we must look at both the individual believer and the broader life of the church, the living stones and the temple being built with them. Unfortunately, discussing the flaws of evangelicalism is like talking to your kids about sex; it is uncomfortable, awkward, and easier left unsaid. Our mothers taught us that polite conversations do not mention politics or religion. We could easily add public schooling to the list of topical taboos because it is the sum of the first two (politics + religion = public schooling). Of course, public educationists strenuously object to that equality—denying secularism, New Age philosophies, and various social engineering curricula are religious and political in nature. But, they are lying; neutrality *is* a myth.

We still reluctantly discuss these issues because they are largely considered private. Our political, religious, and educational ideas are forged in the fires of free will and tempered by personal choice. In America, the right to choose trumps everything including the right to life itself.

We live in an individualistic culture enveloped in an autonomous age, fertile soil for the evangelical doctrines of "soul competency" and the priesthood of the believer (singular). The very idea of absolutes applicable to all believers is regularly discounted in light of the final accountability we owe to God individually. American evangelicals are comfortable with this autonomy; they are not comfortable with uncompromising biblical standards or with admonitions for failing to adhere to them. The evangelical concept of "just me and my Bible" has become so pervasive we rarely unite around creeds, confessions, or even common commitments. To have anyone (including ecclesiastical authority) call us to a biblical standard of Christian education . . . Well, bless your heart, brother; we would rather not talk about it.

How do we approach these things having been taught to fear intolerance, not error? How do we appeal to biblical standards when our Christian brothers differ with us, demanding that all ideas be accepted as equally valid? How do we call believers to universal biblical truths when they recognize no universal biblical authority? Such theological individualism makes it easy to get along, but reduces Christianity to a least common denominator, letting everyone believe anything if they have Jesus in their hearts. And this, for evangelicals, is yet another personal choice. No matter what arguments are presented for Christian education, they can always be dismissed with a wave of an autonomous hand: "Oh, it's nice Christian education works for you, but we chose public schools." Period. End of debate. Discussion closed. Personal choice trumps all. Preference is king.

Although discussing the evangelical "facts of life" is uncomfortable, it is imperative. Yet, we should start with our strengths. American evangelicals have maintained a living faith in the face of historical Christianity's continuing slide toward irrelevance. *USA Today* recently reported the lamentable decline of the church in Europe where the percentage of the population in attendance is now measured in single digits. Americans should ponder this because Europe is our motherland and birthplace of our ideas of democracy, freedom, and faith. Evangelicals should also ponder this because Europe birthed the Reformation and may be a harbinger for the diminution of American Christianity as well. Evangelicalism is at least a speed bump on the road to a post-Christian culture.

Evangelicals have moderately resisted Enlightenment rationalism and the treacherous paths of intellectualism that led many European churchmen away from the flock into higher criticism. This has not necessarily been a conscious effort, but rather a consequence of a more experiential approach to faith and practice. For evangelicals, Christ is concrete, not concept. They emphasize experiencing God, not merely knowing about Him, resulting in a more tangible faith. The term "born again" is laden with life, and evangelicals are often characterized by this vibrant expression.

Over the past quarter-century, evangelicals have presented a more visible cultural engagement as well. They have entered the fray on a variety of political and social issues, becoming the imagined, vast right-wing conspiracy of the imagined, vast left-wing conspiracy. While the lasting impact of this political activity is hard to appraise, evangelicals have undoubtedly exerted electoral influence in the red states liberals refer to as "fly-over" country.

Simultaneous with this resurgence of political engagement, some evangelicals have pursued alternatives to government schooling resulting in the significant growth of Christian schooling and home education. Even so, the percentage of evangelical children receiving a distinctively Christian education remains embarrassingly low.

These examples are sincere accolades for the American evangelical church, which has millions of believers who know, love, and serve the Lord Jesus Christ. Nonetheless, evangelicals are also called to biblical obedience in their personal relationships with Christ. They are not free to define the Christian life on their own terms or pick and choose where and when biblical obedience is required. Thus, areas of apparent evangelical disobedience are germane to understanding the relationship between evangelicalism and public schooling.

When asked point blank which commandment was the greatest, Jesus replied without hesitation, "You shall love the Lord your God with all your heart, and with all your soul, and with all your mind" (Matthew 22:37). Most evangelicals could respond to this, "Well, two out of three isn't bad." We know something about loving God with our hearts and souls, but we do not know much about loving God with all our minds.

We have already established that America has entered a post-Christian era; although we may lament the lack of Christian consensus and influence, the wound is largely self-inflicted. The post-Christian wasteland is the product of the post-Christian mind, for *culture is religion externalized*. In other words, dominant religious beliefs are made evident in cultural expressions. Consequently, religious beliefs underlie the external expressions of American culture.

As Ken Myers points out, ideas have antecedents — how we live determines what we believe. The cultural mediums we integrate into our lives shape our thinking and ideas. Culture, nebulous as it may seem, is a two-way street. It shapes our thinking and our thinking shapes it. Thus, American culture has an insidious and pervasive influence because no matter how ascetic or monastic we may be, we all inhale it like secondhand smoke.

For example, many evangelicals adopt the current cultural mentality of *victimhood*. We embrace an entitlement mentality and whine about the stealing of America: "It's not fair! We have rights; this is a Christian nation." But, nothing has been stolen from us—not our government, not our schools, not our culture, not our families, not our churches, and not our freedoms. We have simply surrendered these things by retreating from biblical thinking in our failure to love God with all our minds. There has been no theft or seizure; secularism and its minions have merely occupied ground Christians have deserted.

Our greatest dereliction of duty has been the education of our children. We have abandoned them deep in enemy territory after sending them ill prepared and ill equipped into a spiritual battle. How dare we act surprised when they are consequently captured, corrupted, and conformed by the world? What did we think would happen when we sent them to be trained in sanctuaries of secularism? This is the point: We did not think. We did not act charitably toward our children. We did not love God with all our minds.

Another carcinogen inhaled from our contemporary culture is our woeful ignorance and disregard of history. Evangelicals think like evolutionists, believing whatever comes later is necessarily better than what preceded it. After all, this is the wireless age of cell phones, email, and everything the World Wide Web offers. We have more information than previous generations, yet our shallow application of truth only mimics the wisdom of our predecessors.

We also disregard our history as the church of the living God. American evangelicals can name more professional athletes than apostles and patriarchs of the faith.

Most of us do not realize the twenty-first century church is a mere shadow of Christendom past. By God's hard providence we live in an age of a weak and anemic church (I am referring to evangelicals, not Catholics, Orthodox, or mainline Protestant denominations, though they often fair no better). We do not hold a candle to our apostolic, patristic, and reformational forefathers. Instead of standing on the shoulders of these giants, we casually dismiss them as irrelevant and anachronistic. After all, we have the Internet!

Many other examples of cultural conformity in modern evangelicals could be cited: our materialism, consumerism, individualism, and pragmatism. In short, the evangelical church has more commonality with the smothering contemporary culture than distinction from it. This conformity to the world is the inevitable result of our failure to love God with all our minds. The apostle Paul astutely addressed this danger in his letter to the Romans: "And do not be conformed to this world, but be transformed by the renewing of your mind, so that you may prove what the will of God is, that which is good and acceptable and perfect" (Romans 12:2).

In his thoughtful book, *Fit Bodies Fat Minds*[1], Os Guinness identifies polarization and pietism as two reasons evangelicals are suspicious of the life of the mind. Polarization is the establishment of false dichotomies in our thinking, severing two things that should be united. Such thinking creates antagonisms between mind and heart, intellect and emotion, faith and learning, and formality and fervor. This sort of polarized thinking falsely pits heart against head. Guinness aptly illustrates this point with dialog from L. Frank Baum's *The Wonderful Wizard of Oz*. It is descriptive of the evangelical mind:

"Why didn't you walk around the hole?" asked the Tin Woodman.
"I don't know enough." replied the Scarecrow,

cheerfully. "My head is stuffed with straw, you know, and that is why I am going to Oz to ask him for some brains."

"Oh, I see," said the Tin Woodman. "But, after all, brains are not the best things in the world."

"Have you any?" inquired the Scarecrow.

"No, my head is quite empty," answered the Woodman; "but once I had brains, and a heart also; so having tried them both, I should much rather have a heart . . ."

"All the same," said the Scarecrow, "I shall ask for brains instead of a heart; for a fool would not know what to do with a heart if he had one."

"I shall take the heart," returned the Tin Woodman; "for brains do not make one happy, and happiness is the best thing in the world."[2]

Thus, falsely thinking we must choose between the two, a majority of American evangelicals have opted for the Tin Man's choice: empty heads and happy hearts.

Pietism is another impediment to loving God with all our minds. It is simply the abuse of piety, the wrong use of a right thing. Piety is a very good thing when undistorted; its noble goal, according to Guinness, is to place wholeheartedness, or total life devotion, at the center of Christian faith and practice. Yet, when the devotion of our hearts is severed from the devotion of our minds, the result is an escapist mentality leading to self-righteous pietism.

Pietism draws us into a self-centered sphere of introverted personal experience where Christianity is reduced to a privatized (often Gnostic) faith. Jesus becomes one-dimensional in pietism—reduced to an ooey, gooey, sticky-sweet sentimental experience. Syrupy pietism makes many evangelicals embark on an endless quest to change their personalities and temperaments with the dubious goal of becoming sweeter than Jesus. We find this engaging, but those around us find it irrelevant.

Desiring to be Christ-like requires much more than imitating His perceived or imagined character traits. The New Testament tells us people responded to more than Christ's personality; they marveled at His wisdom and insight. His parents once found Him in the temple conversing with priests who were astonished at His understanding and answers. He contended with leading religious scholars and lawyers, confounding them with His wisdom. He fed the mysteries of God's Word to everyday people making them marvel at His authority. No doubt many people thought Jesus was a really nice guy, at least when He was not turning over tables and calling them names.

Thus, as Os Guinness notes, "Our evangelical experience has become our strength and our weakness."[3] It is a good thing to love God with all our hearts and souls, but we must also love Him with all our minds. Indeed, it is the greatest commandment that we do so. We must also remember Christ's definition of love, which requires both sentiment and obedience: "If you love me, you will keep My commandments" (John 14:15).

Our disregard of the biblical mandate for Christian education is the defining disobedience in our failure to love God with all our minds. Like our father Abraham, God has chosen us to command our children in the way of the Lord (Genesis 18:19). Indeed, the command to instruct the next generation is a recurrent theme from Genesis to Revelation, and is beautifully expressed in Psalm 78:1-8 as framed in the Scottish Psalter:

> O ye my people, to my law
> Attentively give ear;
> The words that from my mouth proceed
> Incline yourselves to hear.
> My mouth shall speak a parable
> The sayings dark of old,
> Which we have listened to and known
> As by our fathers told.

We will not hide them from their sons
But tell the race to come
Jehovah's praises and His strength,
The wonders He has done.
His word He unto Jacob gave,
His law to Israel,
And bade our fathers teach their sons
The coming race to tell.

That children yet unborn might know
And their descendants lead
To trust in God, recall God's works,
And His commandments heed.
And not be like their fathers were,
A race of stubborn mood,
Which never would prepare its heart
Nor keep its faith in God.[4]

Each generation faces this commandment anew, and ours has kept it poorly by neglecting the doctrine of covenant succession and the biblical command to train our children in the education of the Lord. If we cannot teach our own children to trust in God, recall His works, and heed His commandments, we will never teach a pagan culture to do the same. Such disobedience must surely perish in the wilderness before God will lead His people into the victory He has promised.

Meanwhile, the church is wasting time evangelizing at the front door while its children slip out the back. Christian education is a key to training our children in the way they should go so when they are old they will not depart from it (Proverbs 22:6). Only then will the covenantally faithful become the culturally influential. Brewing up an autonomous, obedience-optional evangelicalism produces a flavor with broad cultural appeal: It tastes great, but is less fulfilling than intended.

It is one thing to examine the influence of evangelicalism in individual believers as this chapter has done. It is quite another to look at the social force of evangelicalism and its influence on the broader culture. That is where we must shift our attention as we continue to examine the bonds between evangelicalism and public schooling. Evangelicalism may be conceived in the heart, birthed in private decisions, and nurtured as a personal faith, but it also has a public face and far-reaching impact on American culture and education.

CHAPTER 7

From Leaders to Bottom Feeders

"If the foundations are destroyed, what can the righteous do?"
— Psalm 11:3

I N HIS 1964 Pulitzer Prize winning book, *Anti-intellec-tualism in American Life*, historian Richard Hofstadter traced the dominant influence of Protestant Christian-ity in the shaping of American society. Hofstadter noted that the Puritan colonies held learning in high regard, par-ticularly among the clergy and the communities they led:

> Among the first generation of American Puri-tans, men of learning were both numerous and honored. . . . These Puritan emigrants, with their reliance upon the Book and the wealth of scholarly leadership, founded an intellectual and scholarly tradition which for three centuries enabled New Eng-land to lead the country in educational and scholarly achievement.[1]

This learned and literary class not only produced enduring institutions like Harvard, but also provided a broader cultural enlightenment that Hofstadter contended, "brought to the New World much of the best of the heritage of European civilization."[2]

Christianity has always felt a certain tension between mind and heart, intellect and emotion. Initially, Puritanism kept a healthy balance between these tendencies, but by the mid-eighteenth century, many established New England churches (Congregational, Dutch Reformed, Presbyterian, Anglican) were drifting toward a dead traditionalism. They maintained religious forms but lacked spiritual power and life.

In the face of this spiritual famine, the First Great Awakening restored much of the faith and vitality of the church, recovering the best of historical Protestant Christianity. God used evangelists and pastors such as George Whitefield, Gilbert Tennent, and Jonathan Edwards to revive true religion and deep repentance within the church. These leaders were learned and impassioned men personifying the greatest commandment: Love God with all of your heart, soul, and mind.

Unfortunately, a far different leadership characterized the Second Great Awakening in the early nineteenth century. Revivalists, such as Charles Finney, reviled churches for their formality and openly attacked their piety, liturgy, and clergy. Instead of reforming the historic churches, Finney traded pulpits for stumps and mesmerized crowds with fiery, emotional, and extemporaneous preaching. Pursuing the miraculous results of the First Great Awakening, Finney and his followers orchestrated man-made revivals using techniques and manipulations designed to be entertaining and reproducible at any time and place. Overall, the revivalism of the Second Great Awakening rejected the historical church and redefined Christianity in an informal religious style convenient to the common man.

The long-established respect for learning in the New England colonies mitigated the mildly anti-intellectual aspects of the First Great Awakening. But, during the Second Great Awakening, appeals to the common man and inflammatory attacks against churches overwhelmed the established religious order. Many historical expressions of Protestant Christianity were abandoned or deformed as once dominant denominations lost ground to revivalist sects. The camp-meeting converts wanted fervor not formality and titillation not tradition. The awakeners correctly rejected formalism and traditionalism, but were wrong to reject *all* forms and traditions. The root problem was the lifelessness of the practitioners, not the practices.

When Christ rebuked the Pharisees — saying they honored God with their lips but not their hearts — He was not complaining about the order of synagogue worship. Jesus regularly participated in their meticulously structured liturgy. The Pharisees were saying and doing the right things, but their hearts were far from God. Christ rebuked them for this hypocrisy, not their formality. Likewise, an unfortunate consequence of the Second Great Awakening was that many forms and traditions of historical Christian worship were abandoned rather than empowered. Indeed, many evangelicals continue to throw the baby out with the baptismal water by tossing their spiritual legacy out with the liturgy.

The abandonment of historical Protestantism for an innovative revivalism paralleled the abandonment of historical educational philosophies for the progressive schooling experiment. Nineteenth-century educators rejected tried-and-true educational paradigms at the same time nineteenth-century evangelicals rejected tried-and-true ecclesiastical paradigms. These iconoclastic cousins were spurred on by the rise of scientism, Darwinism, and popular democracy: Technology will save us; newer is better; and the common man will decide for himself how he worships, is educated, and is governed.

This is not an appeal for a return to formalism and traditionalism, but an appeal for evangelicals to understand what they have rejected and why. The recent resurgence of classical Christian education reveals that nineteenth-century public educators foolishly rejected the very cornerstone of substantive education. Likewise, evangelicals should consider carefully whether nineteenth-century revivalists rejected many things necessary for a healthy and vibrant church. Classical education shows that those who came before knew much more than we thought; the same may well be true of the spiritual predecessors of evangelicalism.

Traditional churches and professional clergy, ill prepared for the tumult of the Second Great Awakening, were also shaken by America's rapid westward expansion. As the nation transitioned to the nineteenth century, the fluid frontier consisted of people often unchurched, uneducated, and uncivilized. The mission of the church to this primitive frontier culture fomented new methods and improvisations by a new breed of minister. Itinerant preachers took religion westward, literally in their saddlebags, to a frontier with little social infrastructure and even less ecclesiastical accountability. They brought a simple message to a simple people, and as Hofstadter noted, "They would have been ineffective in converting their moving flocks if they had failed to share or simulate in some degree the sensibilities and prejudices of their audiences — anti-authority, anti-aristocracy, anti-Eastern, anti-learning."[3] Rapidly, the newly-invented revivalism of the Second Great Awakening became standard frontier fare.

The social force of evangelicalism has perpetuated a legacy that is anti-tradition and anti-learning. By the mid-nineteenth century, Methodists and Baptists, once only dissenting sects, had become the largest Protestant denominations — a testimony to their zeal and effectiveness. Their sweeping gains in believers were evidence of capable adaptation to the changing conditions of American life and the broad appeal of easy evangelicalism. The expansion of evangelical religion continued throughout the nineteenth and twentieth centuries, fostered by revivalist techniques refined in the Second Great Awakening. Evangelists, such as D.L. Moody and Billy Sunday, became point men for an evangelical faith declaring a religion of the heart, not the head. Their rhetoric often echoed the earlier anti-intellectualism of the awakeners.

This exaltation of the unlearned and ordinary man, central to evangelical religion, became the driving force of public schooling. Throughout the nineteenth century, the emerging public schools gradually, yet continuously, shifted instructional focus from intellectual attainment to pragmatic social concerns. The acerbic humor of H.L. Mencken hit close to the mark when he said, "The aim of public education is not to spread enlightenment at all; it is simply to reduce as many individuals as possible to the same safe level, to breed a standard citizenry, to put down dissent and originality."[4]

The caliber of educators available to nineteenth-century public schools made it impossible to teach a rigorous academic curriculum on a mass scale. Many public school teachers had failed at other work or were teaching temporarily. The role of schoolmaster was generally held in low esteem, poorly compensated, and hence unlikely to attract capable persons. Even a century later, with compulsory attendance, standardized teacher training, and extensive public relations, critics like professor Richard Mitchell still castigate the system:

> It is only from a special point of view that [public] education is a failure. As to its own purposes, it is an unqualified success. One of its purposes is to serve as a massive tax-supported jobs program for legions of not especially able or talented people. As social programs go, it's a good one. The pay isn't high, but the risk is low, the standards are lenient, entry is easy, and job security is still pretty good.[5]

Under the pervasive influence of popular democracy and evangelical religion, American public schools became bastions of egalitarian education. Pragmatism and vocationalism dominated curricula formation, and the canon of Western Civilization was diluted to a nearly imperceptible concentration. Commenting on the squandering of our western educational inheritance, journalist Walter Lippmann observed:

> Modern education, however, is based on a denial that it is necessary, or useful, or desirable for schools and colleges to continue to transmit from generation to generation the religious and classical culture of the western world. It is, therefore, much easier to say what modern education rejects than to find out what modern education teaches. Modern education rejects and excludes from the curriculum of necessary studies the whole religious tradition of the west. It abandons and neglects as no longer necessary the study of the whole classical heritage of the great works of great men.[6]

Lippmann's observation is profound: It is easier to identify what modern education rejects than what it teaches. This strikes at the heart of education and makes one wonder if public schools can even function in a multicultural society. *Education is enculturation.* It is the vital link preserving and transferring truth and tradition from one generation to the next. But, what do you pass on in a culture as diverse and heterogeneous as the United States? Education without a unifying cultural theme becomes a jumbled mess of unrelated and disconnected facts instead of a cohesive, integrated, and unified body of truth. Rather than weaving a beautiful cultural tapestry from the threads of knowledge, we twist them into tangles and knots. Thus, they mat and mangle into a pop-cultural hairball instead of interlacing as an intricate social fabric.

When Protestant Christianity was the dominant American religious expression it provided the integration necessary for successful education. A comprehensive body of knowledge, unified by a shared faith, passed from one generation to the next through the education of children. We knew what we wanted children taught and they were taught it. This is not at all the same as knowing what we do not want children taught, and not teaching it. The religious trump card played by the state, allowing only secular religions to be taught in public schools, complicates this further: Secularism is a pathless wasteland without heritage, traditions, or monuments. As a result, public school children act as autonomous arbiters of truth, deciding for themselves what has value and meaning. This is not enculturation or education; it is moral idiocy and cultural self-destruction.

America is now experiencing the deliberate de-Christianizing of its culture; Christianity is no longer the cultural norm and civil common denominator. This is not the normal ebb and flow of religious sentiment, but a tidal shift in cultural perspective pulling the evangelical church into new and uncharted waters. We have long sailed with the assumption Christianity is the prevailing current, but a rapidly growing number of Americans no longer accept Christianity as normative. Many are self-consciously charting a different course.

The loss of Christian consensus has caused a growing cultural disunity and alienation. Public schools exacerbate this cultural segregation, constantly emphasizing our ethnic differences, by their obsession with multiculturalism and diversity. They champion everything from Kwanzaa to Cinco De Mayo, but dutifully ignore Christmas and Easter as the inappropriate cultural baggage of dead, white European males. Ironically, the one thing that unifies cultural diversity is forbidden: It is impossible to resolve the tension between *the one and the many* apart from Trinitarian Christianity. The solution for unifying multicultural

79

diversity is in Christ:

> For even as the body is one and yet has many mem-
> bers, and all the members of the body, though they
> are many, are one body, so also is Christ. For by one
> Spirit we were all baptized into one body, whether
> Jews or Greeks, whether slaves or free, and we were
> all made to drink of one Spirit. For the body is not
> one member, but many. (1Corinthians 12:12-14)

How does this relate to the evangelical church? For nearly
two centuries, much of evangelicalism has dulled the
once-sharp edge of historical Christianity and supported
the Great Dumbing Down Machine: compulsory public
schooling. Yet, these are merely the high points, sparing
the painful details of more recent evangelical excursions
into televangelism, apocalyptic fiction, and weight lifting.
Ultimately, the commissions and omissions of evangelical
Christianity have significantly shaped American life and
culture; indeed, modern America was forged in the fires
of evangelicalism.

Despite our powerful influence, evangelicals are losing the culture war because we fight with the weapons
and tactics of our enemies. We will walk the soles off our
shoes electing another born-again President, while letting
our children be steeped in secularism at the local public school. We build megachurches with seeker-sensitive
worship and attempt to Christianize pop-cultural fads,
and then wonder why Christians are statistically identical
to unbelievers. We whole-heartedly embrace cultural synthesis, but act surprised at the lack of biblical antithesis.

In our desire to reduce Christianity to a single-point
experience, we strip away its cultural context and historical
content. We do not instruct our children in the incredible
riches of their Christian heritage or live our faith in a holis-
tic, integrated demonstration of covenant community. We
sate our children with the junk food of secular schooling

because the shelves of evangelicalism are bare. No wonder Christian kids are often found feeding at the pop-cultural hog trough; after all, the starving will eat garbage. Confronted by cultural and academic malnutrition, renowned educator Leo Brennan offered this recipe for a healthier menu:

> The only solution is to restore the basic educational ideals and principles that provoked Christendom's great flowering of culture in the first place: a strident emphasis on serious and diverse reading, the use of classical methodologies, and all this integrated into the gracious environs of Christian family life.[7]

As the late, great State of Massachusetts legalizes homosexual marriage, it should strike Christians as horribly ironic that our Puritan forefathers first settled there. Despite the evangelical frenzy of direct mailing, telemarketing, and court battles, it is likely the Sodomites will eventually win the day and make this abomination the law of the land. Meanwhile, when will it dawn on hand-wringing evangelicals that public schools have been promoting the gay agenda for decades? Will we wonder, in our shocked pietism, how a majority of people came to the openness, tolerance, and diversity prerequisite to the acceptance of homosexual marriage; or more accurately, prerequisite to the rejection of biblical absolutes?

How did this happen? It was easy; sleepy parents, silent pulpits, and seditious schools taught the next generation to accept Gay and reject God. Evangelicals are nearly helpless to stop this cultural meltdown, but they can only blame themselves. We are like the Crooked Man of nursery rhyme fame—busy walking, talking, and building, yet our lives and labors are twisted and warped. Too many evangelicals have built on sand and now the rains have come.

CHAPTER 8

Where Have All the Christians Gone?

All the evils in our now extensive catalogue flow from a falsified picture of the world which, for our immediate concern, results in an inability to interpret current happenings.
— Richard Weaver

THROUGHOUT THIS BOOK, relationships are implied between school, church, and culture. These entities form a somewhat muddled trio since they possess neither the simplicity of direct cause and effect nor the symmetry of an equilateral triangle. Instead, there are vague influences exerted between them—gravitational forces—in which the orbit of one affects the others and vice versa. It is tempting to oversimplify: Bad cultures produce bad schools, and good churches produce good cultures. These relationships, however, are characterized by nuance and subtlety. Their effects are observable, but the anecdotal evidence is often ambiguous, making it difficult to understand why things are the way they are.

Future historians will see clearly through the fog of provincialism and cultural prejudices surrounding us, but these things obscure our own vision. Yet, as an old adage says, it is better to be approximately right than exactly wrong. Although we may err in being too prescriptive, we should try to gain valuable insights by understanding the times. We may not solve our problems, but we may discover why we have them.

At the risk of leading the witness, I want to engage these ideas through a series of questions. (I do so for two reasons: First, many Christians have never thought about these things and, therefore, have failed to consider important questions. Secondly, it is easier to ask questions than answer them.) Is American culture today more or less biblical than previously? Is the evangelical church in America stronger or weaker than the historical church? If weaker, is it because we have embraced the ideas and practices of cultural decline surrounding us? Or, has the church led the culture into decline? What does history teach about the strength of the church and its cultural influence? In short, which comes first, a weak church or a weak culture?

Christianity is an ancient faith; there is only one name by which men have ever been saved. As the book of Romans declares, those who have faith in Christ are children of Abraham and joint heirs of God's promises to him. Hence, the omnipotent cross of Christ redeems God's elect from Genesis to Revelation, stretching back to Abraham and reaching forward to you and me. Throughout this rich, redemptive history the Holy Spirit has been building what Saint Augustine called the *City of God*.

Many evangelicals naively believe the church began in the 1950s when brother so-and-so came to town with his tent and tambourine. Or they think it was born when a great revival spawned their particular denomination a century or two ago. In reality, men have been saved by grace through faith under God's redemptive plan for more than four millennia, beginning with Abraham—the father of us all (Romans 4:16). Consequently, we possess an incredible legacy in the faithful example of those who walked before us (the great cloud of witnesses of Hebrews 12:1).

Where Have All the Christians Gone?

It is perilous to disregard church history. The children of Israel are part of our Christian heritage. The first-century church is part of our Christian heritage, as is the fifth-, tenth-, fifteenth-, and twentieth-century church, and everything in between. Nonetheless, evangelicals typically trace their roots to the Second Great Awakening or, at best, the sixteenth-century Protestant Reformation. By ignoring thirty-five hundred years of redemptive history, we refuse to learn from the Holy Spirit's leading of our forefathers. Thus, we cannot properly assess our own strengths and weaknesses because we lack perspective and understanding.

What were the commonly held presuppositions of our patriarchal, apostolic, patristic, and reformational forefathers? Were their cultural and ecclesiastical expressions (art, music, literature, architecture, education, commerce, science, justice, worship, etc.) informed by a biblical worldview? Were first-century church and culture more biblically obedient than twenty-first century? What about the fourth, eighth, thirteenth, and twentieth centuries? How do these compare with each other and with us? When has the church walked most obediently? When most woefully? Is the American evangelical church the apex of four millennia of Christian history? Is this the best it has ever been done?

I am not suggesting we ape a previous age out of fear or loathing of our own. Christians should avoid an escapist mentality that longs for an idolized past or an idyllic future. God has providentially placed us in time, and we should pursue the knowledge, understanding, and wisdom necessary for His purposes. Theologian and author J.I. Packer perceptively expounds this point:

> Human nature does not change, but times do; therefore, though the application of divine truth to human life will always be the same in principle, the details of it must vary from one age to another. . . . Application

85

may never be taken over second-hand and ready-made, each man in each generation must exercise his conscience to discern for himself how truth applies, and what it demands, in the particular situation in which he finds himself.

This point is crucial for us who believe that modern evangelicalism stands in need of correction and enrichment of a kind which the older evangelical tradition can supply. It seems that modern evangelicalism is guilty of just this error of living in the past — in this case, in the recent, late-nineteenth century past. We are too often content today to try and get along by re-hashing the thin doctrinal gruel and the sometimes questionable ideas about its ethical, ecclesiastical, and evangelistic application which were characteristic of that decadent period of evangelical history . . .

We certainly need to go back behind the nineteenth century and re-open the richer mines of older evangelical teaching, but then we must endeavor to advance beyond the nineteenth-century mentality into a genuine appreciation of our twentieth-century [and now twenty-first century] situation, so that we may make a genuinely contemporary application of the everlasting gospel.[1]

The church has always navigated among the flotsam and jetsam of non-Christian philosophies and cultures: The paganism of the ancient world, the mythology of Greece and Rome, the superstition and mysticism of the Middle Ages, the humanism and rationalism of the Enlightenment, romanticism, naturalism, existentialism, scientism, environmentalism, feminism, and a host of others have all led to our current post-modern relativism. Finding our way among the reefs and shoals of unbelief is nothing new; what is new, however, is that the evangelical church is floundering.

Historically, the church countered and conquered its enemies by proclaiming the truth in word and deed. We now act as if modern unbelief is so virulent we can no longer know truth. We innovate and capitulate, hoping to reconcile with our enemies. Yet, unbelief, whether individual or cultural, is not the *absence* of belief but the *presence* of belief in lies. Granted, the -*isms* have changed, but unbelief is the same old, hell-bound variety. Men reject light because they love darkness (John 3:19). The church prevails against this darkness by embodying truth and its implications; we must live what we believe and demonstrate what we confess.

Have Christians today lost the ability to evaluate, articulate, and demonstrate biblical standards? In what areas are we called to live in antithesis to the culture around us? In education? In morality? In aesthetics? In worship? Do these things require a restricted and particular expression? Are they matters of personal preference? How intentional and distinctive should Christianity be?

I have intentionally broadened the discussion beyond education to make this point: American evangelicals are often culturally confused. We have forgotten—perhaps were never taught—how to make informed judgments, contextual distinctions, and appropriate applications of our culture expressions. We are surrounded by a post-Christian culture intent on sanitizing itself of all vestiges of Christianity, yet many Christians indiscriminately use this ungodly culture to educate their children, entertain their families, and worship their God.

The evangelical church should be asking how this ecclesiastical wreck can be righted. Russell Kirk correctly identified the starting point, "The culture can be renewed only if the cult is renewed. . . . "[2] In other words, the church must take the beam from its own eye before attempting laser eye surgery on the culture. We need to lengthen our perspectives, abandoning the allure of quick fixes, bold innovative thrusts, and revolutionary tactics. We should ponder today, how to affect our church and culture for centuries. What ministries and priorities will impact our great-great-grandchildren? We must think generationally, and labor longitudinally. As Eugene Peterson wisely instructs, we should pursue "a long obedience in the same direction."

George Grant has remarked that our future is not a Star Trek journey. We are not called to boldly go where no man has gone before. We have no right to redefine ourselves every few years in response to cultural winds of change. Our calling is to be imitative, not innovative; indeed, we are copyists and keepers of God's Word and sacraments. Baptism, Communion, and biblical obedience are the tools of earthly dominion.

Winston Churchill once said, "The greatest advances in human civilization have come when we recovered what we had lost: when we learned the lessons of history."[3] We should look back, not forward, to a church historically healthier, holier, and more culturally influential than we have every dreamed of being. Now is the time for the evangelical church to recover what has been lost. When this is done the cultural tail follow; regrettably, we continue not to do this.

Admittedly these are generalizations, but there are regrettably few exceptions. American evangelicalism is characterized by cultural compromise. The innovative pursuit of cultural relevance by evangelicals has been the surest path to irrelevance. Until Christians recognize that *the church is the problem*, there is little hope of cultural renewal.

We will not have strong churches until we train a generation of children to walk in the truth and wisdom of knowing, believing, and living a biblical worldview. We will not train such a generation if we allow public schooling to sabotage Christian discipleship. Therefore, churches that do not encourage distinctively Christian education are sentencing themselves to a future of impoverished ministry, a dearth of spiritual leadership, and a vacuum of cultural influence.

Like the ancient Israelites, American evangelicals have not separated themselves from those who practice abominations; rather, we have embraced their culture and their gods (Ezra 9:1). We have neglected the instruction of our covenant children by allowing unbelievers to disciple them. When we read those Old Testament stories and wonder how Israel could have been so stonehearted, stubborn, and stupid, we are holding a mirror in our hands.

According to America's egalitarian logic, everyone defines his own religious experience. It does not matter what you believe as long as you believe, or not. Polytheism and consumerism are cohabiting in America, producing offspring of autonomous designer-religions. Some find their savior in Christ, some in crystals, and some in Chryslers. The only unpardonable sin is exclusivity, and the only unpardonable sinner is a biblical absolutist.

Public schooling is the great state church of polytheism. It is here the dogmas of openness, tolerance, and diversity are preached, and the rejection of absolutes deeply ingrained. It is here Christianity must be strictly forbidden because it claims salvation exclusively through Jesus Christ. Without this embarrassingly parochial claim, Christianity might be admitted to the pantheon of gods already worshiped in public schools.

Public schools function as churches by teaching inescapably religious doctrines (e.g., the origin and purpose of man, the nature of the universe, moral philosophy, ethics, and justice) and fostering intentional community among their parishioners. Do public school members need counseling? It's available. Do members need breakfast, lunch, or dinner? It's available. Do members need medical care or family planning? It's available. Do members need childcare? It's available. Do members need transportation? It's available. Nearly all the social and charitable services once provided by church and home are available through the public school and its ugly stepsister, Child Protective Services.

In a bizarre example of over-the-top attempts to proselytize families to the public school church, a school district in Ohio actually gives parents of newborns a Certificate of Adoption by the local elementary school. These infants are optimistically dubbed "Future Readers" and welcomed into the school family *at birth*. When the child begins kindergarten, a baby picture and adoption certificate is posted in the school hallway—a sort of a public school confirmation. Thus, bonds of dependency are formed as public schools usurp the roles historically held by church and family.

Institutional loyalties are formed through the power of shared experience. Where do parents frequently gather with friends and neighbors? Public schools. What drives the family schedule? Public schools. What determines where homes are bought? Public schools. What provides the family with recreational activities and entertainment? Public schools. What gets the most press in the local paper, especially the sports section? Public schools. A smorgasbord of extracurricular activity endears families to the public school, and it works. Public schools have literally become our *alma mater*—our fostering mother.

Evangelical churches, Christian schools, and parachurch organizations would be thrilled to generate the sense of community engendered by local public schools. Christians should feel connected to the cause, supportive of the system, and aligned with the institution—when the kingdom of God is being advanced. But, when an institution like public schooling self-consciously opposes the Word of God, we must not align ourselves with its rebellion. Evangelicals should be as troubled about public schooling as they are about the ACLU, KKK, and Planned Parenthood.

Public schooling has become *the fabric of our lives*, a phrase made famous by a cotton-industry advertisement:

"The touch, the feel, the fabric of our lives." Indeed, public schooling exudes the warmth of a soft, downy comforter. It styles itself as loving, caring, and helping children. It markets itself as the social fabric — the cotton — serving the greater good of children and society alike. How could we live without its comforting caress and kindhearted concern?

Without argument, I grant they labor for the good of children. No one is working in public schooling to intentionally hurt kids. Teachers do not get up in the morning asking how they can deceive their students. (There are plenty of ill motives to be found in public schooling, primarily in the perpetuation of its tax-funded monopoly and bloated bureaucracy. But, I digress.) I do not deny their good intentions; I simply assert that public schools are *asbestos*, not cotton. Clothe your kids in either fabric, but realize one is a carcinogen.

Public schools cut with the grain as they seek to build loyalty and legacy around the power of shared experience — people want to belong. What they fail to deliver in good education they attempt to make up in good will, striving to establish school spirit, alumni allegiance, and community cohesion. In our increasingly irreligious and impersonal culture, public schools are the only semblance of a faith community many people will ever know. This cultural hunger for community and identity allows public schools a nearly cultic influence, engendered through their powerful propaganda machine. Many schools employ full-time, public-relation personnel to promote their image and champion their cause. A myriad of consultants and lobbyists push the public school legislative agenda and peddle tax levies. Lucrative contracts are awarded to local business and community leaders. In short, there are reasons why devotees step forward and drink the Kool-Aid: Their allegiance blinds their understanding, and the benefits flow best when unquestioned.

This fevered loyalty often makes parents more concerned with false starts on the football field than with false teaching in the classroom. Who cares what they teach? The basketball team won the sectional and the football team went to the state finals!

Public schooling becomes a surrogate family, a wedge separating children from parents and siblings. When family ties are rejected for peer connections, many teenagers develop unhealthy emotional dependencies and inappropriate physical relationships through premature romantic involvement. Families find it hard to compete with the lure of friends and the unending menu of school-based activities and entertainment. School psychologists explain this as normal adolescent behavior, as if we should welcome our children's withdrawal from family life as signs of a healthy teenager. The book of Proverbs, on the other hand, attributes this rejection of family authority and cohesion to a sickness of heart and soul.

By artificially grouping children in narrow age groups and processing them lockstep through years of isolation from broader socialization, public schools slowly produce a nearly homogeneous collection of adolescent lemmings. Their conformity and compliance make them indistinguishable expressions of modern American pop culture. These kids wear the same clothes, listen to the same music, watch the same TV, espouse the same values (openness and tolerance), and share the same vulnerability to peer pressure and manipulation.

Under pretense of multicultural diversity, public schools actually create a rigidly monocultural conformity. Amazingly, a country as large and diverse as America produces public school students from coast to coast who are essentially commodities. This is a testimony to the incredible power of shared experience and the coercive nature of public school doctrines. The herding instinct of public schooling and the marketing prowess of Madison Avenue have created something unprecedented: A seductive youth culture whose siren songs compete for the affection, allegiance, and affluence of our children.

Before the advent of public schooling, the church was the predominant center of social and community life. The public school now fills that role; it is the new church. The ecclesiastical nature of public schooling is evident in the rhetoric of its clergy. Public school proponents speak about their ministry with proselytizing zeal. They are true believers in the messianic nature of public schooling; they worship and serve it as society's savior. If describing public school as a church seems an unfair metaphor, ponder these words from one of its prophets:

> I am convinced that the battle for humankind's future must be waged and won in the public school classroom by teachers who correctly perceive their role as the proselytizers of a new faith: a religion of humanity that recognizes and respects the spark of what theologians call divinity in every human being. These teachers must embody the same selfless dedication as the most rabid fundamentalist preachers, for they will be ministers of another sort, utilizing a classroom instead of a pulpit to convey humanist values in whatever subject they teach, regardless of the educational level—preschool day care or large state university. The classroom must and will become an arena of conflict between the old and the new—the rotting corpse of Christianity, together with all its adjacent evils and misery, and the new faith of humanism.[4]

If imitation is the highest form of flattery, the evangelical church and the public school share mutual admiration. Schools have become imitation churches; likewise, churches imitate schools by compelling attendance (through entertainment and attractions) and failing to teach. Ironically, public schools are unconcerned with conversions, but succeed wonderfully at discipling secularists, while evangelical churches are obsessed with conversions, but fail miserably at discipling Christians.

I hope this elaboration over three chapters has supported my allegations that public schooling and evangelicalism are practically kissing cousins. Of course, public schools do not have steeples or crosses. Yet, neither do many churches whose pragmatic, modern architecture increasingly resembles public school buildings.

My arguments assume the implicit nature of public schooling and the religious nature of all cultural expressions: *Education is enculturation; culture is religion externalized.* Those who would dismiss my comparisons of evangelicalism and public schooling must adequately address these observations:

- Both institutions are in the disciple-making business, accomplished by teaching, modeling, and inculcating worldviews.

- Both institutions build communities of true believers through the power of shared experience and the instruction in approved dogma and doctrine.

- Both institutions have been significantly shaped by individualism and popular democracy.

- Both institutions believe in the messianic nature of their message and mission.

- Both institutions concurrently emerged during nineteenth-century rejection of previous paradigms, and have enthusiastically embraced modernity.

- Both institutions disregard the past; evangelicalism and pubic schooling are ahistorical.

- Both institutions have foundations of egalitarianism and pragmatism reinforcing their anti-intellectual structure.

What are the practical consequences of these similarities? Who cares if public schooling and evangelicalism share philosophical DNA? Obviously, this relationship does not negatively affect public schooling; indeed, it has replicated many aspects of evangelicalism and proven better than the church at building a community of believers and producing committed disciples. In other words, public schooling has duped countless evangelicals into supporting its anti-Christian agenda by disguising itself as an angel of light. The real problem, therefore, is not that public schooling operates as a wolf in sheep's clothing, but that evangelicals are unable, or unwilling, to acknowledge this.

Where have all the Christians gone? Many have simply changed churches — it is easy enough to confuse the two.

CHAPTER 9

The Three Rs: Repentance, Reformation, Reading

Deep-rooted customs, though wrong, are not easily altered; but it is the duty of all to be firm in that which they certainly know is right . . .

— John Woolman

GOD MANIFESTS His kingdom through His people; ultimately, the church is the solution, not the problem. The Bible is clear, however, that the church has waxed and waned through periods of triumphant obedience and devastating disobedience. Unfortunately, the latter describes much of American evangelicalism — a difficult truth for evangelicals accustomed to blaming our problems on the world, the flesh, and the devil.

Nonetheless, God remains faithful when we are faithless. Although His judgments visit rebellious men and nations — abortion, homosexuality, and public schooling come to mind — He grants repentance and revival of true religion. We have every reason to be, as George Grant has quipped, "short-term pessimists and long-term optimists." God's promise to the ancient church is true today:

If I shut up the heavens so that there is no rain, or if I command the locust to devour the land, or if I send pestilence among My people, and My people who are called by My name humble themselves and pray, and seek My face and turn from their wicked ways, then I will hear from heaven, will forgive their sin, and will heal their land. (2 Chronicles 7:13-14)

God's people clearly should turn from sin. Yet, it is not some nebulous entity called to biblical obedience; it is you and I. It is easy — too easy — to call for broad corporate repentance based on a nondescript guilt shared by all evangelicals, but we should not sever our individual responsibility and identity from the larger body of believers. Their disobedience is our disobedience, their spiritual health is our health, and their need of repentance is our need — personally. I am saying simply this: Readers should apply the arguments in this book first to themselves and then to the broader Body of Christ.

Many evangelicals, however, are unwilling to begin with themselves. We want a seat at the table — we want to be heard — but we do not want to examine *our* families, *our* children, and *our* lifestyles. We quickly tell others how to live their lives, but reluctantly examine our own. In short, we want cultural influence we have not earned.

This do-what-I-say-not-what-I-do attitude has led to a serious strategic error: Politics as savior. Many Christians equate electoral advantage with spiritual vitality and try to manipulate social change through political machinations — lobbying, telemarketing, direct mail, advertising campaigns, and voter-registration drives. Political means, however, are ultimately inadequate for the needed cultural and ecclesiastical reformation.

Cultural expressions, including the form and function of civil government, are external representations of internal belief — *culture is religion externalized*. The religious faith and practice of its citizens determine a nation's moral character, not the ink of its documents. As a case in point, American courts and legislatures find no inherently Christian implications in our Constitution and now use it to guarantee liberties and rights directly contradicting Christian faith and practice. Documents do not change, but people do.

A predominantly Christian culture will have a predominantly Christian government; a post-Christian culture will not. Although our constitutional federal republic is based on biblical principles — representative government, separation of powers, inalienable rights — it merely preserves and protects prevailing cultural belief. If the culture accepts abortion and homosexuality, these sins will find legal protection and governmental approval. Thus, as Americans increasingly embrace polytheism, relativism, and secularism, these unbiblical beliefs find expression in new cultural forms that enjoy governmental protection — homosexual marriage being a recent example.

Political and judicial battles may temporarily slow the de-Christianizing of America, but evangelicals will ultimately lose the culture war with this strategy. The true battle is for the hearts and minds of men, not for control of Congress, the Supreme Court, or the White House. The necessary reformation is neither easy nor political. We must repent of our sins and turn from our enamored worship of politics. We must learn to love God with all our minds, thinking and acting in a manner consistent with biblical truth.

We foolishly focus on electing a few Christians politicians while millions of new voters graduate each year, saturated in the post-Christian cultural agenda taught in public schools. Political activism is a ridiculously ineffective strategy for building Christian culture; but public schooling is a brilliant strategy for subverting it. It is spiritual schizophrenia for Christians to champion conservative political efforts while simultaneously sending their children to public schools. Why do Christians do this? They do not think through the biblical implications of their actions. Like Aaron, whom God appointed to lead His people out of bondage, we are found presiding over the casting of a golden calf.

Evangelicals must recover the slow, consistent plodding of daily Christian living: loving our spouses, serving our families and friends, building meaningful relationships, enjoying our work, studying God's Word, training and equipping our children via thoroughly Christian education, and pursuing substantive worship in local churches. We should be about the business of building intentional community in our homes, churches, and cities. These are the seeds of reformation; the plants that grow from them will bear the fruit of cultural transformation.

These suggestions are not glamorous or revolutionary; indeed, they are reformational and generational. Unfortunately, the delayed gratification inherent in reformation frustrates impatient evangelicals. "Read books?" they moan, "Build relationships? Who has time for that? We want to make a difference now!" So we join more groups, serve on more committees, and champion more causes. We are in church every time the doors open, but cannot remember the last time our families spent an evening at home together (with the TV off). Life dashes past in a frantic blur of overcommitment, underachievement, and dissatisfaction. We respond by doing more.

Our lives come to resemble a dry lakebed — smooth, widespread, and efficient for setting land-speed records. Yet, not a single seed can take root, grow, and flourish in this arid, compacted earth. We desperately need to slow our pace, prepare the soil, and plant seeds of change. We must then patiently nurture the tender growth until it bears fruit of personal, ecclesiastical, and cultural renewal.

Some may consider the last 'R' an unlikely vehicle for change, but *reading* is the workhorse implement of repentance and reformation. This seemingly simple activity requires time, thought, and discipline. It can be difficult

100

and demanding but yields delightful rewards: It plows the fallow ground of cultural conformity and renews our minds. Indeed, the apostle Paul described its power as, "...the washing of water with the word" (Ephesians 5:26). This metaphor of sanctification refers specifically to reading Scripture, but a general principle applies: Reading nourishes the soul.

For this reason, parents should strive to model a life-long love of reading. Children learn from our example; not every lesson requires a plan and syllabus. I sometimes jest a teenager's greatest fear comes true: They become their parents. Although we flinch to see our weaknesses mirrored in our children, we should recognize the incredible power of a positive example. The formative power of parental example has tremendous implications for education. The truth is simple: If our children know learning is important to us, it will be important to them. Of course, for our love of learning to be convincing, our children must see us reading substantive books, not just cultural chaff such as sports magazines, pulp fiction, and daily newspapers.

Perhaps the first question we should ask is, Why read? It is a good question with several good answers. I like James Schall's concise reply: "Why read? Because we are given more than we are."[1] Despite our hyperactive self-esteem there are many things twenty-first century Americans do not know. We casually disregard what came before or exists outside of us. We inexplicably believe ourselves the smartest people ever to have graced this planet — primarily because the other guys are dead.

Reading — particularly old books — lends proportion to our warped contemporary perspectives. This is a desperate need, because America at the dawn of the new millennium is not the apex of Christian history; the church is a shadow of its former glories. We are neither the best nor brightest, and worse, we are woefully ignorant of who those were. We live downwind from the fires of neglect that have ravaged the old growth and tall timber of our spiritual and cultural heritage. We stand with smoke in our eyes and our shoulder in the wind of more than one hundred and fifty years of educational conflagration.

A dysfunctional public schooling system only perpetuates our cultural confusion. Stepping out of this prison to breath fresh air—free from the stifling conformity of public school orthodoxy—one begins to taste the difference. The greatest educational challenge many parents face is giving their children what they never received themselves: an academically rigorous, morally excellent, and biblically integrated education. Propelling our children further than ourselves is never easy, but parents who have found alternatives to public schooling often comment, "My kids are finally getting the education I never had."

As Christians take direct responsibility for their children's education and walk away from government schooling, they must avoid smug self-confidence and false praise. Doing it better than public schools is no achievement at all. Outrunning an invalid is not something to brag about. If we want to make comparisons to high educational standards, we must look to those who preceded us.

We are now far down a steep slope of ecclesiastical, educational, and cultural decline. We have lost our footing and have long been sliding in the post-Christian shale. As we survey the ruins around us, the task of rebuilding seems overwhelming. It will be slow and difficult; the uphill trek is never as easy or as fun. Lest we despair, we must acknowledge a sovereign God has providentially placed us here to make a difference—we were born for such a time as this.

If we are to find and follow a path out of our pervasive and decadent cultural decline, we will have to find it in books, not in TV or mass media. Reading and studying the greatest book, the Bible, is obviously paramount. But we also need to read broadly from the great books of the past. C. S. Lewis explained why:

> Every age has its own outlook. It is specially good at seeing certain truths and specially liable to make certain mistakes. We all, therefore, need the books that will correct the characteristic mistakes of our own period. And that means the old books. . . . People were no cleverer than they are now; they made as many mistakes as we, but not the same mistakes. They will not flatter us in the errors we are already committing; and their own errors, being now open and palpable, will not endanger us. . . . The only palliative is to keep the clean sea breeze of the centuries blowing through our minds, and this can be done only by reading old books.[2]

An appeal for cultural renewal through historical understanding may seem too philosophical and intangible as a motive for reading. Will reading old books reform the church, change the culture, and renew education? Well, yes, sort of. Reading will not bring an immediate, drive-thru, fast food kind of change Americans expect. Reading changes us slowly and thoughtfully. It is a tool of reformation, not revolution, vital in the long, slow process of building intentional community, recovering substantive education, and transforming the broader culture.

Reading allows us to fill our minds in obedient response to Paul's instruction, "Finally, brethren, whatever is true, whatever is right, whatever is pure, whatever is lovely, whatever is of good repute, if there is any excellence and if anything worthy of praise, let your mind dwell on these things" (Philippians 4:8). Filling our minds with truth by studying the Bible and great literature will help us escape the bondage of our modern "Egyptian" pop culture that so easily enslaves us. We must avail ourselves of God's deliverance: Reading lights the path out.

Indeed, the words of a modern-day Moses to our generation might well be, "Let my people read."

I cannot leave this topic without admonishing Christian parents: Read to your children. All of us can and should read aloud to our children regularly. Reading aloud is vital to their educational and moral development. By reading together children soon discover the joy and appreciation of good literature. They learn to listen, imagine, and visualize a story. They get a feel for the rhythm, texture, and cadence of words. They experience the emotive power of language, and receive a clear parental message that reading is very important. "Never underestimate the power of books for children." Richard Ogilvie wisely advised, "Note this well: it was the literature we read before we attained sophistication, maturity, and adulthood that has done the most to mold our characters, frame our thoughts, and influence our lives."[3]

CHAPTER 10

What Now?
Finding the Path Out

If you don't care where you're going, it doesn't make a difference which path you take.
— The Cheshire Cat (Alice in Wonderland)

WISDOM IS THE calculus of knowledge; its complexity means there are many difficult questions this book cannot answer. We want simple answers, checklists, and acceptable excuses, but these are rare. It is clear, however, that choosing the public school path like everyone else is an unwise, simplistic solution.

One of the worst things Christian parents can do is subject their children to public schooling when they are young and defenseless. The greatest damage from public schooling often occurs in elementary years because these are so developmentally critical — spiritually, socially, and scholastically. The common misconception that public schools are safe at the elementary level has lured many families into a downward spiral. Children enter kindergarten carefree, cute, and curious, only to exit sixth grade cool, aloof, and afflicted with academic deficiencies.

Parents who send young children to public schools often consider pulling them out of middle school, junior high, or high school to spare them from sex, drugs, and rap music. We should protect our children, but the primary threats to their well-being are internal, not external. By seventh grade, a child is already halfway through the systematic secular programming and worldview indoctrination. When concerned Christian parents tell their budding middle-schoolers they will soon be attending We're Not Cool Christian School, the results are predictable. Public schooling has captured their hearts and minds during supposedly innocuous and innocent elementary years. To their dismay, many parents discover by the time their already peer-dependent children hit middle school, "It's all over but the shouting."

Oddly enough, this easy apathy toward public schools often reverses as Christian children near college age. One of the current evangelical ironies is the great importance placed on Christian colleges after casually dismissing Christian elementary and secondary schools as unnecessary. Parents seem to wake up suddenly at thirteenth grade and decide their kids need protection from worldly philosophies and immoralities. Oops, too late! Many parents belatedly send their children to evangelical "monasteries" — complete with legalistic, externally imposed, draconian pietism — knowing all too well twelve years of public schooling have left their children unable to recognize or counter a non-Christian idea if it slapped them in the face. Their kids are untrained and unequipped to engage an unsaved world.

Unfortunately, by college age the bad fruit parents worry about is already ripening from seeds planted as far back as kindergarten. Children equipped with a thoroughly Christian education are more than a match for the non-Christian lifestyles and philosophies they may encounter in college; children equipped with a thoroughly agnostic education are not. Many Christian leaders champion this "college only" approach to Christian education, but it is simply too little, too late.

This does not mean parents should be unconcerned about what colleges and universities teach. Even at Christian colleges, mandatory chapel and pietistic dress codes are no guarantee of biblical worldview in the classroom. Religiously affiliated colleges can be as steeped in relativism and secularism as the state schools where their professors were trained. Wise Christian parents should be more concerned about Charles Darwin, Karl Marx, and Sigmund Freud than about Hugh Hefner, Adolph Coors, and Phillip Morris. More importantly, these concerns must begin in kindergarten, not college.

A common rationalization parents make is that their neighborhood public school is somehow an exception to the general rot in American education. The convenient, free, "Facilities-R-Us" public school down the street is always attractive because it has resources we covet: sports programs, enrichment classes, and a bevy of extra-curricular activities. Our friends and family members attend or work in these schools, and we pay taxes for these opportunities. This affection for public school trappings reveals a fundamental ignorance among Christians regarding what education is (enculturation) and its primary purpose (discipleship). Misunderstanding our educational direction, we wrongly assume public schools are headed the right way. We mistake as parallel, paths that are perpendicular, and we confuse as common, destinations that are worlds apart.

British educator Charlotte Mason perceptively described education as an atmosphere, a discipline, and a way of life. Many Christians are finding her observation — *education is life* — increasingly evident. After wandering the wasteland of secular schooling, they have discovered firsthand that a godless education is a lifeless education. They are survivors of a forced march in which the meager academic rations were highly processed to ensure complete dehydration of all living water. In contrast, Christian education offers a fulfilling banquet of art, history, music, science, literature, and liberty; a veritable promised land awaits those who escape the public school wilderness. These incredible riches are the legacy and inheritance of a distinctively Christian education.

The philosophy and methodology of Christian education imparts an appreciation for permanent things. Providing a thoroughly Christian education for our children involves much more than offering a safer campus and smaller classes than public schools: It is nothing less than the recovery of what has been lost. Through substantive Christian education we stand on the shoulders of giants and reclaim an invaluable legacy. Sadly, too few parents guide their children to these verdant pastures because they have not sojourned there themselves. It is hard to envision a rain forest if you have never left the desert.

Once again, *education is enculturation*. All schools incubate ideas, beliefs, and philosophies. Every school teaches its students presuppositional beliefs about God, man, and the created order. These beliefs may be overt or covert, but they are never nonexistent. Our parental responsibility is to ensure our children receive the rich, vibrant, and full-orbed educational legacy bequeathed on them by centuries of Christian thought and practice. How dare we trade their birthright for a bowl of public school potage?

Children not long exposed to public school have the greatest opportunity of recovering their education. If your children have traveled far down the public school path, however, their foundation is set and the concrete nearly dry. At this late stage, intervention should be built on prayerful petitions for God's grace and mercy in their lives. It is never too late, but it does become increasingly difficult to escape. The conflict may not be pretty.

If your children are still young and responsive to your authority, you must do everything possible to provide a thoroughly Christian education. If at all possible (It is much more possible than you imagine.) you must remove them from public schools. Here again, wisdom is complex. A knee-jerk reaction to pull your child out of second grade tomorrow because he learned the F-word today is not a principled decision. You must read, investigate, and understand your options and responsibilities. Some situations may mean not going back tomorrow, others may mean leaving at the end of the grading period, semester, or school year.

Within the boundaries of God's providence, parents must take direct responsibility for their children's education and ensure that it is thoroughly Christian. All educational decisions should be based on principled obedience to the Word of God. It is not enough to recognize and reject the bad fruit of public schooling. We must be proactive, not reactive, or we will do the right things for the wrong reasons. Reactionary decisions lack the staying power and conviction necessary to sacrificially provide our children a thoroughly Christian education. Reactionary parents often return to public school when they find Christian education too hard, inconvenient, or expensive.

For this reason, parents must understand why public schooling produces bad fruit. Public schools produce non-Christian beliefs and behaviors because they are based on non-Christian doctrines and philosophies. Put succinctly: *Public schooling is actively and intentionally non-Christian.* This is not to say public schooling produces abject pagans; indeed, the opposite is true. According to research by University of North Carolina professor Christian Smith, public school students consistently espouse a religious faith he defines as, "Moralistic Therapeutic Deism."[1] This public school faith bears a shadowy similarity to Christianity but posits its theological tenets without particularities:

- god (small G for generic) whoever he, she, or it is, exists.

- god made the world (presumably by evolution) and takes care of things.

- god is a cosmic therapist; you call him when you need him, otherwise, he leaves you alone.

- The purpose of life is to be a nice person — happy and good.

- There is a heaven and all good people go there.

- Almost everyone is good.

In short, be nice, be good, be happy, and everything will be fine. Such "faith" is a far cry from biblical Christianity whose theological particularities (e.g., sin, justification, election, redemption, forgiveness, and sanctification) are embodied in the atoning work of Jesus Christ. Public schools are not comfortable with tangible definitions. Instead, they steep students in a pluralistic civility making them unwilling to express any belief others might find intolerant. Public schools teach children to deal with moral disagreement and ethical arguments by avoiding them; they believe it is better to be morally inarticulate than appear socially intolerant.

Moralistic Therapeutic Deism is often mistaken for Christianity, and many parents hold these heretical beliefs. No wonder they contentedly leave their children in public schooling. These parents do not discern the dangers of this doctrinal error and even reinforce it at home. Consequently, children almost always lose the spiritual battle they encounter in public schools. Pushed into the ring by their parents, they are soon disarmed by a congenial claim of neutrality, only to be sucker-punched and pummeled with left-right combinations of secularism and deism. Few children go the full twelve rounds without their faith being knocked out or severely injured; many simply concede the fight early in the bout.

Unfortunately, placing your children in the nearest Christian school is not necessarily the solution. By biblical standards, no public school is good, but regrettably, many Christian schools are not either. Evangelicals are still taking baby steps in the recovery of quality education, and many Christian schools are emulating the public school model instead of developing distinctively biblical philosophies and methodologies. The lack of quality Christian schools is one reason for the prevalence of home education.

Parents often have few choices. Even if they are fortunate enough to have access to a quality Christian school, the enculturation of children remains a parental responsibility. Doug Wilson wisely cautions parents against abdicating their educational responsibility, regardless of their schooling choice:

> Parents who have their children enrolled in a Christian day school are responsible to see that the cultural weight of the family is dominant in how their children are educated. This cannot be done by just dropping off the kids and tuition check. The involvement of parents must be active and it must be constant. The same care must be taken if the family is homeschooling. Abdication is possible anywhere, including a homeschooling situation with an absentee, detached father.[2]

Parents must realize that leaving public schooling is countercultural and difficult; indeed, many things mitigate the rejection of public schools. Yet, the greatest enticement of public schools — financial convenience — is an illusion. They are free only at the point of entry. Through payroll deductions and escrow impounds, we hardly notice the thousands of dollars paid annually in property tax, income tax, and bond millage. Many families pay the equivalent of private school tuition in public school taxes, but do not realize the premium they are paying for inferior and defective schools. One can imagine the outrage if every taxpayer sat down once a year and wrote a check to the local public school for a few thousand dollars. Instead, the educational phlebotomists bleed them slowly.

Many Christians cannot afford to walk away from public schools because they are unwilling to make the financial sacrifice. When the mortgage, car payments, and credit cards demand more than we make, the truth of Proverbs 22:7 is clear, "The borrower becomes the lender's slave." By pursuing a lifestyle beyond our means we shackle ourselves to public schooling. Considering home education or private schooling requires a real—often painful—cost-benefit analysis. Unfortunately, many Christian parents exchange their convictions for comforts. Worse yet, those who do not compromise find little encouragement for thrift and sacrifice from either culture or church.

An apt metaphor of public schooling is the fabled Philistine giant—Goliath. Like public schools, Goliath was an intimidating and powerful force: gigantic, pagan, and defiant of the living God. Had he triumphed, God's people would have been conquered and enslaved. Likewise, yielding hearts, minds, and children to the public schooling colossus enslaves Christians today; trusting God and giving children a thoroughly Christian education sets them free.

Goliath was defeated by the seemingly foolish and weak: a ruddy youth, a slingshot, and a stone. Arrogant public school giants may mock our small, faltering steps toward Christian education. Let them laugh; someday they, too, will fall before the living God, either willingly or beneath a millstone. Until then, Christian parents must not hide among the rocks and cower before the bravado of these self-proclaimed giants of learning.

Those who criticize the *status quo* are often accused of negativity. A lady once scolded me for being against public schools instead of for them; she thought I ought to do a better job of brightening the corner where I live. Nonetheless, my criticisms are not the hapless ramblings of a pessimistic crank, and I do not despair for the future of education or the church. I optimistically anticipate the collapse of the government-schooling monopoly because I believe Americans are too resourceful to continue this failed social experiment indefinitely. It may die slowly, or it may surprise us and fall apart suddenly like the former Soviet Union under the weight of its own dysfunction and absurdity. Either way, we should welcome its demise, busy ourselves removing the rubble, and build distinctively Christian educational opportunities on the ruins.

We should also be full of faith concerning the future of the church. The church has the Word and the Spirit—the *promise* she will be cleansed, sanctified, and presented as a spotless bride, and the *empowerment* to become a glorious church, holy and blameless (Ephesians 5:25-26). Our disobedience does not thwart the plan and promise of God, though He chastens us as a loving father disciplines his children. G.K. Chesterton once remarked, "Faith is always at a disadvantage; it is a perpetually defeated thing which survives all conquerors."[3] In the same way, the church will certainly survive this Age of Relativism and its cultural confusion. The question is whether our generation will perish in the wilderness, longing for "Egypt," or possess the land by faith, repentance, and obedience.

I wish leaving public schools was the silver-bullet solution for what ails us. I do believe public schools are a major cause of our cultural and spiritual illness; leaving them is one key to the recovery of healthy families and strong churches. Our evangelical disobedience, however, is broader and more complex than this. We must honestly examine our lives in the shadowless light of biblical truth. Our marriages, child-rearing, finances, work, education, recreation, relationships, and worship must conform to the lordship of Christ. In other words, pulling your children out of public schools is a great first step; it is fruit in keeping with repentance (Matthew 3:8). But, we dare not stop there. We must sincerely question why we do what we do and actively bring our multifaceted lives into comprehensive obedience to the Word of God.

This is not a small responsibility, but recent developments are greatly encouraging. Parents who want alternatives to our current cultural and ecclesiastical inanity are not alone. Nearly two million American children are now home educated, and the number continues to grow. Millions more attend Christian schools. Major evangelical denominations openly debate the use of public schooling. Christian parents are increasingly aware of the worldview conflicts inherent in government schools. Evangelicals are also rethinking many modernist assumptions that shape contemporary life. Consequently, there is renewed interest in establishing meaningful covenant communities and recovering historical expressions of church, family, and education. Those seeking the path out of our current confusion will find it clearly marked—it is becoming well traveled.

Education as enculturation is the *leitmotif* of this book, yet I do not expect readers to recognize and accept it blindly. Books journeying into rough terrain and unfamiliar territory cannot be adequately evaluated in one pass. Unfamiliar scenery demands more attention of the reader, so I encourage you to re-read this book, now knowing the lay of the land. Susan Wise Bauer offers similar advice to all readers:

> To tackle . . . reading successfully, we have to retrain our minds to grasp new ideas by first understanding them, then evaluating them, and finally forming our own opinions. ...It is impossible to analyze on a first reading; you have to grasp a book's central ideas before you can evaluate them. And after you've evaluated—asking, "Are the ideas presented accurately? Are the conclusions valid?"—you can ask the final set

of questions: What do you think about these ideas? Do you agree or disagree? Why? [4]

Although your next reading will be quicker, I urge you to make underlines, highlights, and margin notes. These travelogues will help recount the journey and your impressions along the way. Ultimately, you will arrive at your opinions through paths of contemplation, understanding, and evaluation; finding these less-traveled ways requires more than one trip through the territory.

Others have written more helpful how-to books on Christian education, and I gladly refer readers to the recommendations in Appendix A. It contains much of value for planning an escape from public schooling and much to contemplate regarding Christianity and culture. The importance of further reading is evident, for as Mark Twain once mused, "The man who does not read good books has no advantage over the man who cannot read them." [5]

Admittedly, I do not have all the answers. I have, however, seen hundreds of Christian parents successfully transition from public schooling to Christian schooling. Their efforts have not been easy, but they have been extremely rewarding. These parents have had the delight of renewing parent-child relationships, seeing their children grow in Christian virtue and character, and recovering strong academic achievement. The vast majority of these families would never go back to government schooling. Nevertheless, you — the Christian parent — must ultimately decide for or against Christian education, for you bear the responsibility and consequences of this choice.

This book is a WARNING SIGN marking a detour on the educational highway. Its bright orange barricades and flashing lights may startle some readers, and annoy others. Some will ignore it, careening onto the dilapidated bridge of public schooling without edge lines or guardrails. Others, having seen the detour sign, now sit on the roadside pondering what to do; I sympathize with them. The alternative routes seem longer and more difficult; indeed, they actually lead to a different destination. These routes are less familiar and less traveled; some appear newly constructed, and others are ancient paths. The broad road is full of hazards and dangers, but the narrow road seems risky too — what should parents do?

As you consider the journey ahead think first of the final destination: *an academically rigorous, morally excellent, and biblically integrated education for your children.* Many paths may lead to this objective, but you must begin by deciding where to end. Resolve to give your children a thoroughly Christian education, then consider the options for getting there.

Some parents take the home education path, others, Christian schools, and some, a combination of the two. They travel these roads in various curricular vehicles, reflecting parental choice of educational philosophy and methodology. We should be encouraged, not intimidated, by the diversity of ways to achieve a thoroughly Christian education. Although we do not share identical methods, it is wise to learn from others who journey toward the same goal.

It is also essential to rest along the way. We need to pause for fuel, food, and fellowship with our fellow travelers; we should discuss the road ahead, the prevailing weather, and the maintenance of our educational vehicles. To this end, a strong, supportive church is vital to sustaining our educational drive. Pastors and congregations who intentionally promote Christian education invaluably help us reach our final destination. It is much harder to travel alone and be told at every rest stop to turn back.

An inquisitive Alice once asked, "What is the use of a book without pictures or conversations?"[6] I ponder the same question as I close this book aware of its inadequacies. I have tried to paint vivid pictures and beckon readers to the Great Conversation of the ages. Immodestly, I hope

116

this book will find its way into the hands and minds of many Christian parents and give flower to a healthy dissatisfaction with the evangelical and educational *status quo*. Lord willing, dissatisfaction may become disenchantment, breaking the spell under which many slumber. We must continue in hope of this awakening: "Awake, awake, put on strength, O arm of the Lord; Awake as in the days of old, the generations of long ago" (Isaiah 51:9).

God neither sleeps nor slumbers, and His Word declares this promise to the church: "God is in the midst of her, she will not be moved. God will help her when morning dawns" (Psalm 46:5). May a new dawn of educational understanding and evangelical obedience break forth soon.

Reading Recommendations

Most ignorance is vincible ignorance; we don't know because we don't want to know; we remain uninformed because we refuse to read."

— Aldous Huxley

KNOWING WHAT TO do is easier than doing it, and reading is not an exception. We certainly have good intentions: Some books we intend to buy but never do, others we buy but never read, and far too many we start but never finish. Our modern love affair with the electric plug (and the entertainment it powers) robs us of the time and temperament necessary for reading. We live in an age where the visual image — immediately accessible and seductively alluring — has triumphed over the printed page.

"When I am dead," Hilaire Belloc once quipped, "I hope it will be said: His sins were scarlet, but his books were read."[1] Regrettably, it is likely unread books will be added to our list of scarlet sins, for reading is a spiritual discipline modern Christians have too long neglected. Our appetite for Elysian electronics, coupled with the intellectual wounds suffered in public schools, bars us from the treasury of books.

Public schools have taught legions of students not to love reading. These students are conditioned to associate books only with school, as if they leave books and learning behind at graduation. It is a shame on us that videotapes, DVDs, and CDs often outnumber our books. One recent survey indicated the average college student has seen a hundred movies for every book read. This is the fruit of a culture and educational system imparting a love of entertainment rather than a love of learning. Books and education are not the special prerogative of public schools; indeed, these institutions are impediments to a learned and literate society, as evidenced by the excessive remediation required by colleges, employers, and post-secondary training centers.

Public education consistently fails to impart a love of learning. If public schools trained pilots, they would graduate with no desire to fly. Although airplanes are valuable in training student pilots, they are far more useful in the hands of experienced aviators. Likewise, books are useful in training children, but are invaluable to adults. Sadly, "I don't read books" is an epithet fitting too many public school graduates.

It is especially important for Christians to read. God specifically sanctions a high regard of books by revealing Himself in the Bible. Ultimately, our names must be found in books if we are to enter into eternal life (Revelation 20:12).

"It is a man's duty to have books." Henry Ward Beecher admonished, "A library is not a luxury, but one of the necessaries of life. Be certain that your house is adequately and properly furnished—with books rather than with furniture. Both if you can, but books at any rate."[2] Toward this end, I have outlined a lecture by George Grant listing ten steps for establishing an invaluable habit of reading.[3]

Reading Recommendations:

1. **Read widely.** Do not be too specialized. Read from a broad range of topics and styles.

2. **Read deeply.** Read books that are hard for you. Read important books that challenge and stretch your thinking.

3. **Read outside your own time.** Escape the smothering conformity of our contemporary popular culture by reading books from other times and cultures.

4. **Read classically.** Read the books that, through historical and continued acclaim, form the canon of essential reading for any well-educated mind.

5. **Read with purpose.** Develop a plan. Make a list. Write it down. Keep a journal.

6. **Read aloud to your kids.** Remember the best children's books are the ones adults like the most. If a child's book seems absurd and boring, do not inflict it on your child.

7. **Read & buy quality books.** The medium is nearly as important as the message. When possible, buy new or used hardback editions instead of paperbacks. Begin to build a family library with quality hardbound books.

8. **Read down the footnote trail.** Where did your favorite authors get their inspiration? To what books do they refer? One good book generally leads to another. Search them out and read them.

9. **Read in a specified place.** We have dedicated places

for TV and eating, why not books? Create a designated place in your home conducive to quietness and reflection, devoted to reading and studying. Building a family library can be one of the greatest educational inducements you ever undertake. It models a love of learning and leaves a legacy for future generations.

10. **Read enjoyably.** Make Anthony Trollope's words true for yourself, "This habit of reading, I make bold to tell you, is your pass to the greatest, the purest, and the most perfect pleasures that God has prepared for His creatures... It will make your hours pleasant to you as long as you live."[4]

Recommended Reading:

I have quoted from many books (listed in Appendix C) well worth your time and attention. In addition, the following books specifically elaborate on the themes of education, culture, and the church. This list is not exhaustive and is offered only as a convenient guide to readers who desire further study and understanding.

Critiques of Public Education

1. Bruce Shortt, *The Harsh Truth About Public Schools*

2. Chris Klicka, Homeschooling: *The Right Choice*

3. Douglas Wilson, *Excused Absence: Should Christian Kids Leave Public Schools?*

4. Joel Turtel, *Public Schools; Public Menace: How Public Schools Lie To Parents and Betray Our Children*

5. John Taylor Gatto, *Dumbing Us Down; The Underground History of American Education*

Classical and Christian Education

1. C.S. Lewis, *The Abolition of Man*

2. Douglas Wilson, *Recovering the Lost Tools of Learning; The Case for Classical Christian Education*

3. Jessie Wise and Susan Wise Bauer, *The Well-Trained Mind: A Guide to Classical Education at Home*

4. Steven C. Vryhof, *Between Memory and Vision: The Case for Faith-Based Schooling*

5. Susan Hunt, *Heirs of the Covenant*

Lifelong Learning

1. Gladys Hunt, *Honey For A Child's Heart*

2. James V. Schall, *Another Sort of Learning*

3. Louis Cowan and Os Guinness, *Invitation to the Classics: A Guide to Books You've Always Wanted to Read*

4. Susan Wise Bauer, *The Well-Educated Mind: A Guide to the Classical Education You Never Had*

5. Terry Glaspey, *Great Books of the Christian Tradition*

Culture and Christianity in America

1. Christian Smith and Melinda Lindquist Denton, *Soul Searching: The Religious and Spiritual Lives of American Teenagers*

2. Ken Myers, *All God's Children and Blue Suede Shoes: Christians & Popular Culture*

3. Nancy Pearcey, *Total Truth: Liberating Christianity from Its Cultural Captivity* (especially Part 3: How We Lost Our Minds, Chapters 9-12)

4. Neil Postman, *Amusing Ourselves to Death; Technopoly: The Surrender of Culture to Technology*

5. Os Guinness, *Fit Bodies Fat Minds: Why Evangelicals Don't Think and What To Do About It*

Websites of Interest

1. Alliance for the Separation of School & State: www. honested.com

2. Canon Press: www.canonpress.org

3. Classical Christian Homeschooling (CCH): www. classical-homeschooling.org

4. Considering Homeschooling Ministry: www.consideringhomeschooling.org

5. Escondido Tutorial Service: www.gbt.org

6. Exodus Mandate: www.exodusmandate.org

7. Home School Legal Defense Association (HSLDA): www.hslda.edu

8. Mars Hill Audio Journal: www.marshillaudio.org

9. National Association of University Model Schools: www.naums.net

10. The Association of Classical & Christian Schools (ACCS): www.accs.edu

11. Veritas Press: www.veritaspress.com

12. Vision Forum: www.visionforum.com

13. WorldNetDaily: www.worldnetdaily.com

14. Rescue Your Kids: www.RescueYourKids.com

15. Discover Christian Schools: www.discoverchris-tianschools.com

The Path from Gath

Time that's lost, displeases those who know
Its precious worth was squandered long ago—
Days wasted in the tutelage of fools,
Spent grinding water in the public schools.

State churches, these, who neutrally decree
Fallacious faith through creed and liturgy
Bereft of Christ and built on man alone—
A stumbling block and soon a neck's millstone.

Yet boast these public priests the noble claim,
"For the children!" (they have blinded and made lame).
They labor so to fire the darkened coals
"For the children!" (they have stunted in their souls).

But save your breath the parents to adjure,
No warning signs will they find harbinger.
They let the siren song their hearts beguile,
And forsaking leadership become servile.

Though clearly shown the error of their way
And told their children there are led astray,
They reminisce upon the schools they're from
And glibly add, "But they would miss the prom!"

Rich legacy entrusted to this bunch
Is soon discarded for the state's free lunch.
From beauty, truth, and goodness they're set free
Through multicultural diversity.

And children having gifts with stick or ball
Are seldom given any choice at all.
Such kids are cheered for racing toward a goal,
Fleet feet esteemed more highly than their soul.

The warning from our pulpits is but pale.
They care not that the children worship Baal?
And yet express both shock and disbelief
When faith and virtue fall before the Thief.

Thank God a band of brothers gives us hope,
Such families as from public schools elope.
And pay a double-tax for public scorn,
Misunderstood as those untimely born.

Suspicion from both church and state alight.
The only crime is thinking we are right
To train our children in the way to go—
The idols of our culture to bring low.

Advantage seems to favor those from Gath,
For Christian education is a path
Less traveled, due to rocks along the way—
Stones slowly smoothed to fit a sling someday.

The church is weak and much about her ill.
In such an age we live by His good will.
So we should always hope for extra innings,
And trust His Word "Despise not small beginnings."

— Bradley Heath

Notes and Works Cited

Preface

1. Hector Hugh Munro, "Down Pens" from *The Complete Saki* (New York: Viking Penquin, 1982).

2. Robert Louis Stevenson, *Familiar Studies of Men and Books* (London: Chatto & Windus, 1905), p. ix.

Chapter 1
Fooled by the Familiar, Enamored by the New

1. Dante Alighieri, *The Divine Comedy, The Inferno, Purgatorio, and Paradiso* (New York: Pantheon Books, 1948), p. 69.

2. John Buchan, as quoted by Grant, *Letters Home* (Nashville: Cumberland House, 1997), p. 63.

3. Ibid., p. 63.

4. Susan Hunt, *Heirs of the Covenant* (Wheaton: Crossway Books, 1998), pp. 47–48.

5. G. K. Chesterton, St. Thomas Aquinas, *Collected*

Works of G. K. Chesteron, Vol 2 (San Francisco: Ignatius Press, 1986), p. 465.

6. John Taylor Gatto, *Dumbing Us Down*, 2nd edition (Gabriola Island, BC: New Society Publishers, 2002), p. 11.

7. Wilfred M. McClay, *Do Ideas Matter in America?* from *The Wilson Quarterly*, Summer 2003, p. 77.

8. Douglas Wilson, *Standing on the Promises* (Moscow, ID: Canon Press, 1997), pp. 94-99.

9. Allen Bloom, *The Closing of the American Mind* (New York: Simon & Schuster, Inc., 1987), p. 61.

Chapter 2
Things We Would Rather Not Know

1. Susan Hunt, *Heirs of the Covenant* (Wheaton: Crossway Books, 1998), p. 121.

2. T. C. Pinckney, "We Are Losing Our Children," Remarks to the Southern Baptist Convention Executive Committee, Nashville, TN, September 2001.

3. Slogan from the ad campaign for Virginia Slims cigarettes, circa 1968.

Chapter 3
Teaching Is Evitable, Learning Inevitable

1. C. S. Lewis, *God in the Dock – Essays on Theology and Ethics* (Grand Rapids: William B. Eerdmans Publishing, 1998), pp. 115–16.

2. Ibid.

3. G. K. Chesterton, as quoted by Hunt, *Heirs of the Covenant* (Wheaton: Crossway Books, 1998), p. 137.

4. Russell Kirk, *Redeeming the Time* (Wilmington, DE: Intercollegiate Studies Institute, 1998), p. 11.

5. Allen Bloom, *The Closing of the American Mind* (New York: Simon & Schuster, Inc., 1987) pp. 25–26.

6. C. S. Lewis, *God in the Dock – Essays on Theology and Ethics* (Grand Rapids: William B. Eerdmans Publishing, 1998), p. 93.

7. Ken Myers, *Mars Hill Audio Journal*, Volume 68, May/June 2004.

Chapter 4
Rise Up, O Men of God

1. Abraham Kuyper, as quoted by Grant, Lecture to the Christian Home Educators of Ohio (CHEO) Conference, June 1998.

2. Ken Myers, *Mars Hill Audio Newsletter*, December 2003.

3. Ibid.

Chapter 5
School Reform: Dress Codes for Strip Clubs

1. Douglas Wilson, *Standing on the Promises* (Moscow, ID: Canon Press, 1997), pp. 93–94.

2. David Bruce Hegeman, *Plowing In Hope* (Moscow, ID: Canon Press, 1999), p. 16.

3. Ibid., p. 15.

Chapter 6
Christian Lite: Tastes Great, Less Fulfilling

1. Os Guinness, *Fit Bodies Fat Minds: Why Evangelicals Don't Think and What to Do about It* (Grand Rapids: Baker Book House Co., 1994).

2. L. Frank Baum, *The Wonderful Wizard of Oz* (New York: Justin Knowles Publishing Group, William Morrow and Company Inc., 1987), pp. 57–58, 61.

3. Os Guinness, *Fit Bodies Fat Minds: Why Evangelicals Don't Think and What to do About It* (Grand Rapids: Baker Book House Co., 1994).

4. Psalm 78, vv. 1–8, from the Scottish Psalter, 1650.

Chapter 7
From Leaders to Bottom Feeders

1. Richard Hofstadter, *Anti-intellectualism in American Life* (New York: Alfred A. Knopf, 1963), p. 60.

2. Ibid., p. 61.

3. Ibid., p. 80.

4. H. L. Mencken, as quoted by Richman, *Separating School and State* (Fairfax, VA: The Future of Freedom Foundation, 1994).

5. Richard Mitchell, *The Leaning Tower of Babel* (Boston: Little, Brown and Company, 1984).

6. Walter Lippmann, *The State of Education in This Troubled Age*, Vital Speeches of the Day, January

15, 1941.

7. Leo Brennan, as quoted by Grant, *Shelf Life* (Nashville: Cumberland House, 1999), p. 193.

Chapter 8
Where Have All the Christians Gone?

1. J. I. Packer, *The Puritans and the Lord's Day* from *The Puritan Papers* (Phillipsburg, NJ: P&R Publishing, 2000), pp. 88–89.

2. Russell Kirk, *Redeeming the Time* (Wilmington, DE: Intercollegiate Studies Institute, 1998), p. 10.

3. Winston Churchill, as quoted by Grant, *Lost Causes* (Nashville: Cumberland House, 1999), p. 20.

4. John Dunphy, "A Religion for a New Age," *Humanist*, January-February, 1983, p. 26.

Chapter 9
The Three R's: Repentance, Reformation, Reading

1. James Schall, *Another Sort of Learning* (San Francisco: Ignatius Press, 1988), p. 29.

2. C. S. Lewis, *God in the Dock – Essays on Theology and Ethics* (Grand Rapids: William B. Eerdmans Publishing, 1998), p. 202.

3. Richard Ogilvie, as quoted by Grant, *Shelf Life* (Nashville: Cumberland House, 1999), p. 168.

Chapter 10
What Now? Finding the Path Out

1. Christian Smith, Melinda Lindquist Denton,

Soul Searching: The Religious and Spiritual Lives of American Teenagers (New York: Oxford University Press, 2005).

2. Douglas Wilson, *Standing on the Promises* (Moscow, ID: Canon Press, 1997), p. 12.

3. G. K. Chesterton, as quoted by Grant, *Lost Causes* (Nashville: Cumberland House, 1999), p. 122.

4. Susan Wise Bauer, *The Well-Educated Mind* (New York: W. W. Norton & Company, 2003), p. 19.

5. Mark Twain, as quoted by Grant, *Shelf Life* (Nashville: Cumberland House, 1999), p. 154.

6. Lewis Carroll, *Alice's Adventures in Wonderland* (New York: Random House, 1946), p. 3.

Appendix A
Reading Recommendations

1. Hilaire Belloc, as quoted by Grant, *Shelf Life* (Nashville: Cumberland House, 1999), p. 106.

2. Henry Ward Beecher, as quoted by Grant, *Shelf Life* (Nashville: Cumberland House, 1999), p. 66.

3. George Grant, "Building a Library of Excellence," Lecture to the Christian Home Educators of Ohio (CHEO), June 1998.

4. Anthony Trollope, as quoted by Grant, *Shelf Life* (Nashville: Cumberland House, 1999), p. 24.

Acknowledgments

We few, we happy few, we band of brothers.
— King Henry V (William Shakespeare)

T his book is more than I am. It is a synthesis and sharing of many lives. I hope those mentioned by name are comfortable with this association, though I do not speak for them. I am also sincerely thankful for some names I do not mention, whose sympathies lay elsewhere; I would never have written this book without their disagreement.

I am very grateful for Tari—the companion and love of my life. Wife, mother, and home educator, she has implemented the ideas that were often only mental play for me. She has endured my obsessing over the ills of public schooling and, with immeasurable patience, has allowed me to work on this book while certain remodeling projects in this old house remain unfinished.

George Grant is one of my heroes and I have gleaned much from his lectures and books. I am thankful for Doug Wilson and the many publications of Canon Press. Ken Myers, and his insightful Mars Hill Audio Journal, has helped me contemplate culture, community, and Christianity. Fritz Hinrichs brought classical Christian education to my doorstep through his excellent Internet-based, Great Books tutorials; my family will be forever grateful.

I owe a debt of gratitude to Patch Blakey (The Association of Classical & Christian Schools), E. Ray Moore Jr. (Exodus Mandate), and Marshall Fritz (Alliance for the Separation of School & State). Their early encouragement, continuing enthusiasm, and final endorsement helped bring this project to fruition.

Randy Dell, Ken Jones, and Steve Keiter sat in my library on numerous Tuesday nights teaching me the importance of friendship, fellowship, and farming. Although the latter is not a topic for this book, we beat many plowshares into swords discussing the merits of agrarian life amidst a culture that is increasingly characterized by narcissism, gnosticism, and numskullism.

Cathy Duffy, Audree Heath, Ken Jones, Wade Lineberger, Mark Shaw, Bruce Shortt, Todd Stollberg, and Tom Thistleton provided invaluable editorial review. Their faithful wounds challenged my arguments, corrected my grammar, and generally provoked me to do my best on behalf of the reader. I am indebted to their honest friendships, generous encouragement, and insightful recommendations.

Tom Askew is a kindred spirit. He was a cool stream in my desert years, and I still find his friendship, humor, and wisdom refreshing. He remains my particular friend and I thank him for his editorial assistance and for writing the Foreword to this book—much herein lived first in our conversations. *Non nobis Domine non nobis sed nomini tuo da gloriam* (Psalm 115:1).

Brad Heath
Wilmington, Ohio
Saint Crispin's Day 2005

Kudos for
Millstones & Stumbling Blocks

Unlike other books advocating Christian education, *Millstones* confronts the practical and theological errors of the evangelical church in abdicating the education of children to the government schools. Families persuaded of the necessity of Christian education will find useful points of dialogue for helping others understand and commit to Christian schools or home education. Heath's analysis of the cultural and moral consequences of rejecting Christian education and embracing public schooling is among the best yet written. If the trumpet gives an uncertain sound who will prepare for battle? Heath sounds a clarion call for the evangelical church to commit to Christian education as part of their walk of faith and obedience.

E. Ray Moore, Jr.
Chaplain (Lt. Col.) USAR Ret.
Founder and Director, Exodus Mandate
Author of *Let My Children Go*

There is no greater failing among Christians than our lack of obedience in the education of our children. We must stop offering our children up as living sacrifices to the Moloch of government schools. Whether we make the necessary sacrifices to provide our children with a Christian education will determine whether future generations bless us for bringing about a spiritual and cultural renewal or curse us for allowing a once great Christian nation to slide into darkness. Brad Heath understands the stakes and eloquently points the way.

Bruce Shortt
Attorney, and author of *The Harsh Truth about Public Schools*

What's wrong with coveting my neighbors' wealth for educating my children? Most people in my church call it entitlement, not coveting, but does it still violate the Tenth Commandment? If you can handle a paradigm threat with a whiff of humor, read Brad Heath's *Millstones and Stumbling Blocks*.

Marshall Fritz
President, Alliance for the Separation of School & State

Brad Heath has entered the growing arena of authors justifiably condemning the government school system. Before you say, "Oh, no! Not another one!" remember that the apostle Paul wrote, "To write the same things to you, to me indeed is not grievous, but for you it is safe" (Phil 3:1). Christian parents with children in the government school system can't receive Brad Heath's hard, pointed, and piercing message often enough. Contrary to the firmly held but false beliefs of many Christian parents, the government school system is not a blessing from God, but rather, a millstone about the neck of our nation, and more specifically about the neck of the children that the Lord has entrusted to the diligent care of their believing parents. As Brad Heath aptly points out, "We did not know this" will not be a satisfactory response from parents when called to give an account for giving their children up to "Caesar."

Patch Blakey
Executive Director
The Association of Classical & Christian Schools

About the Author

BRADLEY HEATH IS an impassioned advocate for the recovery of substantive Christian education. Raised in rural Indiana, he graduated from Purdue University as an aeronautical engineer and has worked in commercial aviation in California, Arizona, and Ohio. Heath has been an active member of the evangelical church and has served as an ordained elder and a Christian school administrator. Brad and his wife, Tari, have been married for twenty-five years and have three children—all classically home educated.